ROUTLEDGE LIBRARY EDITIONS: THE ADOLESCENT

Volume 17

THE HAWKSPUR EXPERIMENT

THE HAWKSPUR EXPERIMENT

An Informal Account of the Training of Wayward Adolescents

W. DAVID WILLS

LONDON AND NEW YORK

First published in 1941 by George Allen & Unwin Ltd, second impression 1967

This edition first published in 2023
by Routledge
4 Park Square, Milton Park, Abingdon, Oxon OX14 4RN

and by Routledge
605 Third Avenue, New York, NY 10158

Routledge is an imprint of the Taylor & Francis Group, an informa business

ISBN: 978-1-032-37655-4 (Set)
ISBN: 978-1-032-38045-2 (Volume 17) (hbk)
ISBN: 978-1-032-38052-0 (Volume 17) (pbk)
ISBN: 978-1-003-34323-3 (Volume 17) (ebk)

DOI: 10.4324/9781003343233

Publisher's Note
The publisher has gone to great lengths to ensure the quality of this reprint but points out that some imperfections in the original copies may be apparent.

Disclaimer
The publisher has made every effort to trace copyright holders and would welcome correspondence from those they have been unable to trace.

The Hawkspur Experiment

An informal account of the training of wayward adolescents

by

W. DAVID WILLS

London

GEORGE ALLEN & UNWIN LTD

RUSKIN HOUSE . MUSEUM STREET

FIRST PUBLISHED IN 1941
SECOND IMPRESSION 1967

PRINTED IN GREAT BRITAIN
in 11-Point Fournier Type
BY PHOTOLITHOGRAPHY
UNWIN BROTHERS LIMITED
LONDON AND WOKING

TO

STUART PAYNE

Preface to the First Edition

EARLY in 1935 I had an article in *The Friend* (the weekly paper of the Quakers) calling for bolder experiment in the treatment of young offenders. Shortly afterwards I had a letter from Dr. Marjorie Franklin informing me that she was convener of a small group of people who had much the same approach to this problem as myself, and asking me to meet them. I did so, and shortly afterwards joined the Q Camps Committee, the aim of which was "for training in a free environment on sympathetic and individual lines, young people who—mainly through environmental causes—present difficulties in social adjustment or have been in unfortunate circumstances (whether or not they are actual lawbreakers)."

This organization was still in an embryonic stage, and we decided to start our work when we had £1,000, in addition to the loan of a piece of land.

We started Hawkspur Camp in May 1936, though we had only (so far as I remember) some eight or nine hundred pounds, and the land we had been offered on loan was no longer available, so that we had to spend some £500 odd in buying land. I was offered—and accepted—the post of Camp Chief. We remained chronically short of funds and by January 1940 the war had made it impossible to continue the work we had so far been doing, though the Q Camps Committee is still in existence and is working with evacuated children.

This book is the result of those four years, but is by no

means to be taken as a complete account, official or otherwise, of the work of Q Camps. Rather it is a personal confession of faith, largely illustrated by cases and incidents from our experiences during those years, as well as by a certain amount of autobiographical material. Yet it is in a way an account of those four years—sketchy, incomplete, thrown together in the odd moments of precarious freedom from an exacting task, and an attempt to expound the principles on which that work was carried out. I hope there will one day be an exact, scientific, and polished assessment of what we did at Hawkspur Camp—that must come from other pens than mine. In the meantime I present this inadequate picture of it as I saw it.

Although the first person singular will frequently recur in what follows, the work which was done at Hawkspur Camp was a co-operative effort. As Camp Chief I was necessarily the pivot around which the work of the camp revolved, and in this work I owe a tremendous debt of gratitude to my colleagues of the staff, who endured much discomfort and financial insecurity in seeing our ideals come to fruition. In particular I must express my deep sense of debt to the two who were longest with us—Mr. T. C. Bodsworth and Mr.A. T. Barron, known to us all, and to the readers of this book, as "Bods" and "Bunny."

But I was, if Hitler will allow me to say so, only one end of an axis. At the other end was Dr. Marjorie Franklin, round whom revolved all the paraphernalia of administration, finance (though she always said she would have nothing to do with that), publicity, and treatment. And by treatment I mean the assembling of men and means to help us in the medical, psychological, and research aspects of our work.

Preface

What Q Camps owes to Dr. Franklin can never be assessed. As this is so I will not risk failure by attempting it. I will be content with recording the fact.

But we had tremendous help from others (though Dr. Franklin was nearly always the channel through which they came to us). Dr. Denis Carroll brought to our aid the resources of that admirable organization the Institute for the Scientific Treatment of Delinquency, as well as the inspiration of his own personality and the help of his counsel, which was inspired by rich experience and wide learning.

To our Chairman, Cuthbert Rutter, to Dr. Norman Glaister, to Miss Craven of the Howard League, to many scores of sympathetic friends and helpers, I owe more than I can say. If the work which they were able to do through me seems to them to have been of any value, I hope that I need not use mere words to assure them real sense of gratitude for their loyal help and constant encouragement.

I need hardly say, of course, that the names of inmates which occur throughout this book are entirely fictitious. In general it may be assumed that when the same person is referred to more than once the same pseudonym is used. But in one or two cases, where it was more than usually important to "screen" identity, I have mixed two or more people's histories, though not in such a way, I believe, as to invalidate any conclusion I may have drawn. It must also be said that nowhere do I attempt a complete clinical picture of any case. Incidents and pieces of case history are drawn upon freely, but only to illustrate specific points. I should not like it to be thought that the point I happen to be illustrating by any particular case was ever regarded as constituting the whole of that particular case, though I must confess that I have sometimes made it seem so.

The work of Hawkspur Camp, then, revolved round an axis with Dr. Franklin and the Committee at one end, and me and the camp at the other. But I wish to make it quite clear that no one but myself bears the slightest responsibility for anything that is said in the following pages. The work of diagnosing the members of the camp was carried on by the Selection and Treatment Committee, which was composed mainly of medical psychologists. Much of what I may say about the interpretation of symptoms in specific cases may be derived from discussions at that Committee, but again, much of it may not, and while I am anxious that my colleagues should have the fullest recognition of all their help I do not want them to be blamed for any false doctrine that may appear between the covers of this book. For I am not a psychologist. I am that most noxious of creatures, a layman dabbling in psychology. Although I may refer to psychological phenomena and attempt to draw conclusions from them, I must here make it clear that I speak not as a psychologist or as a scientist, for I am neither. I speak, if I must put myself in a category, as a Christian. For while I believe the work we were doing to be based on sound scientific principles, my own interest in our methods was primarily that they were in keeping with what I conceive to be the teachings of Jesus. But the Q Camps Committee were not committed to that view, and I can therefore saddle them with no measure of responsibility for what is written here. I can only ask them (so far as they are medical people) to forgive the errors and gross misconceptions of a layman, and thank them very warmly for the opportunity they gave me of doing a very thrilling piece of work. I only wish I had the skill to make a record as thrilling as the experience.

One other acknowledgment needs to be made. Hitler's axis recently acquired a third pole. Mine has had three all along. In this book I am pleading for more Q Camps, but I am not sure that I am not crying for the moon. If any group of people attempt it they will say, "The great thing is to get the Right Man." They will be wrong. The great thing is to find the man with the right wife. And I very seriously doubt whether there is another.

There is a certain hackneyed phrase which one often sees in the early pages of books. Only now do I realize what depth can lie in those commonplace words. They should appear in this book, for they are true of it. But in this case it goes beyond the mere written record—"but for her, this work could never have been done."

Preface to the Second Edition

It is more than 25 years since this little book was first published, and it has long been out of print. The reissue now is at the instance of the Planned Environmental Therapy Trust, who believe this to be an appropriate moment at which to remind the public of our pioneer venture of 30 years ago.

They believe this time to be appropriate because there is a large and growing concern with the problem of crime and its treatment, arising not only from the obvious increase in crime and social maladjustment, but also from a changing climate of opinion about the whole subject.

What we were doing at Hawkspur was new and it was unique. It was (as Dr. Marjorie Franklin has stated elsewhere) not merely a conglomeration of "good ideas" each of equal value without the others, but the careful simultaneous use of a number of interlocked instruments whose total effect was far greater than the sum of its constituent parts.

This has not been tried again. It is true that several of our instruments have since found favour separately. Many who have never heard of Hawkspur Camp have heard of Outward Bound and similar projects. Group therapy may be said to have had its early beginnings at Hawkspur Camp, though our sessions were—by design—not self-consciously therapeutic in intention. Shared responsibility too has come to be experimented with in all manner of places, and few workers with maladjusted children are now unaware of the need to work through good affective relationships.

But we believe that the value of what we tried (in very inauspicious circumstances) to do was in the combination of techniques and instruments adding up to a definite system or method, which we have come to call Planned Environmental Therapy. The war killed Hawkspur Camp. Perhaps the time has come for another look at what we tried to do, and another attempt by other people to do it.

The book has perhaps many stylistic crudities, and I dare say there are some things which, if I were writing it today I would express somewhat differently, but there is nothing I would want to unsay, and what I believed then in my thirties I believe no less firmly now in my sixties. Indeed, the remarkable thing about the Hawkspur Experiment, and the reason my colleagues and I believe it to be worth while to re-issue this account of it, is that in its ideas and its methods —worked out in detail by the Q Camps Committee before I joined them—it is still thoroughly up to date.

One of the distressing things about that four years at Hawkspur was that—although we were doing the kind of thing and doing it in the kind of way that is now gaining a large degree of acceptance—it was all so little understood in those days that we had great difficulty in getting social agencies to refer men to us. By the same token, if a man was referred to us, it was difficult to get anyone to maintain him financially. The result of all this was that we often succumbed to the temptation to accept men who were not really suitable for our kind of treatment. Some of them really needed intensive psycho-therapy. Some proved to be in the early stages of schizophrenia, and so on. Again, it was only to be expected that maladjusted people would display their symptoms in the course of treatment, but if that display took the form of a delinquent act, it was not easy to persuade the Courts to allow us to continue treatment by letting the man return to the Camp. In view of all this, the degree of success we had was quite remarkable. I am not in touch—after thirty years or so—with many of the men, but it may be of interest to the reader if I record what I do know about the after-histories of the men referred to by pseudonym between these covers.

Adrian. Page 176. Self-condemned as "an ineffectual intellectual," and by others condemned as irretrievably workshy, Adrian now has two degrees and is engaged in literary research.

Tom Beeley. Pages 24, 47–50, 113 and 114, 161–165. The spineless good-for-nothing is now senior sales representative of a large industrial concern. He took me out last year to a magnificent expense account kind of dinner, and told me that he still has a little trouble with the old man, who gets more fractious as he moves towards senility; but none with the girl he married against his father's will, and with whom he has lived happily ever after, being now proud grandparents.

Bryn. Pages 128 and 9, and 151, 155 and 157. Contracted a fatal illness and died shortly after the original edition was published.

Arthur Ford. Page 69. Joined the Army early in the war, and was on that troopship (or was it ships?), that arrived at Singapore just in time to go straight into a Japanese prison camp. He was never heard of again.

Edward Gough. Pages 40, 167–71. Edward was as I said "a competent wage earner for two years" and indeed for several more. Then he felt the need for further psycho-therapy, and submitted himself to someone who had been one of the Camp's honorary psychiatric consultants. This helped him for a time, but I later heard that he was in a psychiatric hospital, and I have now lost touch.

Slosher Hare. Pages 53, 94–6. No news since he joined the Army, but I am perfectly confident that his troubles were over.

Sidney Harman. Pages 110–12, 126, 127. No news since he came to see me during the war, when he seemed all right.

Charlie Horsfall. Pages 53, 55, 56, 118–21. A respectable middle aged married man, who has been employed by the same Local Authority for the last twenty years. When he came to the camp at the age of 25 he had been pretty well given up as hopeless.

Roland Leaf. Pages 42, 45. No news.

Mac. Pages 76–86, 141–4. No news since he came to see me during the war in the uniform of an R.A.M.C. corporal.

Reggie Male. Pages 147–8. I heard shortly after the war that Reggie had trained as an occupational therapist and married a colleague.

Tom Miner. Pages 66, 67, 88, 89. "Marched and fought with the Eighth Army" and survived, since when no news.

Tod Orange. Pages 20–2, 42. No news, but I am confident that Tod's no news is good news.

Cuthbert Parsons. Pages 149, 171, 172. I have had intermittent contact with Cuthbert, who now in his middle fifties, does residential work with maladjusted children.

Jim Payne. Pages 27, 28, 40, 138, 188. Alas, I lost touch with Jim just after the war. He too served in the western desert, was wounded, came on leave to find his home and entire family destroyed by a land mine. Married and settled down, and I feel pretty sure, lived happily ever after, but I lost him about 1950.

Raymond. Pages 126–8, 130–3, 145 and 6, 178, 179. Public opinion has now pretty well caught up with Raymond, who, after incredible experiences during the war and shortly after, eventually established a menage with another man of artistic leanings, with whom he has lived for the last fifteen years.

Preface

Hans Schmidt. Pages 53, 54. After serving during the war as a Commissioned officer (one of the few enemy aliens to do so) settled into a successful business career.

Willie Watson. Page 136. I do not even remember who this was.

The Planned Environment Therapy Trust, mentioned above, was founded in 1966 to facilitate further study of the kind of methods used at Hawkspur Camp. Its present activities include the provision of consultative and therapeutic services to residential establishments; funding selected students on advanced courses of study related to P.E.T.; financing research; providing holding stocks of relevant books and publications for sale; providing speakers for conferences and training courses, and publishing a journal '*Studies in Environment Therapy*'.

Further information about the activities and publications of the Trust may be obtained from P.E.T.T., New Barns School, Church Lane, Toddington, Glos. GL54 5DH.

Contents

CHAPTER ONE

The Common Cause

"He's a good boy really . . ."
ANY MOTHER

THERE were six of us, and all our eyes were on one person. A lean, gaunt figure, he came across the brow of the hill and descended towards us across the clover field. In one hand he carried a bulgy suitcase, in the other a cumbersome parcel which afterwards proved to be an ornate paraffin lamp.

"Welcome to Hawkspur Camp. You are our first member."

"Are you the Warden?"

"I am David Wills. This is Dan Minton, the Deputy Camp Chief. Walter Smith, who's going to show us how to grow our own vegetables. Ron Urwin—Roy Gibson—we call them Student Helpers. Ron's going to show us how to erect our own buildings. Roy will show you which tent you're to sleep in—that's my wife."

"I am actually the first member then?"

"Yes, the very first. We've been here a week now getting things ready. We've put up the tents, as you see; we've got to know our neighbours, and we've put in three hundredweight of potatoes. Now we're ready for you and those who will come after you. But you are the very first, and you're going to help us make history."

Our first member. He had "committed" himself. Buffeted about, kicked from pillar to post since his parents deserted him as a baby, misunderstood and mishandled, he had become at the age of twenty-three one of society's "misfits." Reading in the paper of the new "Q Camps" that were going to give fresh hope to people like himself, he applied for admission—and here he was.

We have welcomed about fifty since that day. Some, like him, coming of their own volition, others "sent" by courts, probation officers, social workers, doctors, parents. But all having this in common—that they were conscious of their failure to fit in with what society had expected of them, and they wanted to start all over again.

At Hawkspur Camp they found something they had been seeking all their lives and the lack of which had often been a major cause in bringing them there. They found approval. Approval, not necessarily and always of their acts, but always of themselves. The Cockney mother who went to the police court to plead for her son put it in a nutshell. "He's a good boy, yer honour, bar what he does."

We believe that of all of them—and we act on it.

"Yus" is perhaps a typical example. "Yus" was tough. Seventeen years of age, he had been brought up by poor but respectable parents, but had got in with a tough crowd at the street corner, and had for the time being accepted their values—was seeking their approval. Why he could not or would not accept the standards of his parents' circle I never found out. We used to call him "Yus," because that was almost all he said for the first few days. He wore a scarf round his neck, and a scowl on his face, and quite obviously did not know what to make of us. He simply knew that what matters is whether you're tough, so he scowled and grunted and spoke in monosyllables. We are not tough (in his sense at least) at Hawkspur, so we didn't challenge his toughness. We smiled at him and called him by his Christian name, but we didn't take very much notice of him. At first he clearly despised us as a lot of softies, but he soon began to notice things. Among other things he noticed "Bunny" Barron, who runs the construction squad. Bunny is no more tough than the rest of us. He doesn't believe in hitting people, and he actually reads poetry! But he could swing a shovel in the concrete mix just as well as our tough young friend, or a little better, and could work wonders with a hammer and chisel. "Yus" began to unbend. He joined the construction squad, and in a few months began to reveal an entirely different temperament—the one his mother was thinking of when she told the court "he's a good boy really"—gentle, considerate, sensitive—and most important, he was happy. At the end of six months he was actually attending the Poetry group! I do not mean that a miraculous change had taken place in the boy's personality in the short space of six months. I merely mean that after six months the tough crust had begun to crack in places, and the real "Yus" showed itself from time to time. We knew it would take a long time yet for the crust to disintegrate altogether. So this story is not invalidated by its sequel. One day, while Bunny was on holiday, "Yus" made the acquaintance of a "tough guy" and two days later was persuaded to assist in the burgling of the local pub. He was sent to Borstal, and whether they will ever discover the "Yus" we were beginning to dig out I don't know. I am inclined to doubt it.

Their mothers nearly always tell the court "He's a good

boy really." The court good-humouredly says, "Just so, just so," and then proceeds on the assumption that she's wrong. But she isn't. What she means is that, she *knows*, in spite of his stealing, and lying, and truancy, he does really want to find acceptance by the people among whom he lives and moves. He does—really—in spite of all the appearance to the contrary, want to win approval. So he's a good boy really. What she may not realize is that she, or some other person who is important in his young life, has failed to make him realize that he is approved.

If we are to achieve spiritual maturity, we need to be loved, as we need food and drink if we are to achieve physical maturity. If we cannot find approval in the home, we shall seek it elsewhere. "Tod" Orange is a case in point. He was a charming lad, if you like 'em that way. He had a wicked twinkle in his grey eyes, a cheerful grin on his face, and if there was fun or mischief afoot he was never far off. His father died before he was born, and when his sister was about two. His mother was an admirably well-meaning woman, but gifted with little intelligence and less humour. (If ever the "unfit" are sterilized, those without humour should be dealt with first as unable to rear children satisfactorily.) Girls she felt she knew all about. She had been one and therefore obviously knew how to deal with Eileen. But boys are another problem. She had never been a boy, and all she knew about boys was that they need discipline or they run wild. She entered then with trepidation and misgiving on the task of bringing up Tod. As soon as he began in the mildest way to show a little spirit, the vessels of her wrath—in the interests of discipline—were emptied upon him. Incidents which, in Eileen's development met with a calm and reasonable response from mother, in Tod produced maternal agitation and distress. Tod very soon—even if not quite consciously—began to draw comparisons. He seemed to be denied something which Eileen received. She was loved and approved and he was not. Children can see a good deal more than many adults imagine, but it is too much to expect Tod to understand that his mother is frightened of him. He perceives that however hard he tries he can never secure the approval that Eileen has. It is not surprising that lacking rewards he became weary in well-doing, especially when he found that there was reward of exactly the kind he wanted, applause, approval, acceptance, from the boys on the corner, for certain exciting but illegal activities. So, at the age of sixteen, he came to Hawkspur Camp. We had no difficulty in approving him as soon as we saw him—he was a very attractive youth. He fastened himself on to Bods (my colleague, T. C. Bodsworth, Bursar, Quartermaster and general factotum) who became a substitute mother for him, and the very slightest reproach from Bods would send him off into tears. Even so, he still wanted his real mother's approval. He went home for a week's holiday, and came back in a very bad temper. When he had been back a fortnight I received a letter from his mother asking if all was well, as she had heard nothing from him since he had written to say he was ill in bed. As he had been about as active as an unbroken colt ever since his return I felt that something here was not as it should be. It was not difficult to fathom. Tod had been home, had been nagged by his mother for a week while Eileen enjoyed perfectly amicable relations with her. Coming back to Hawkspur disappointed and disgruntled, he hit upon a brilliant idea. If he was ill, then his mother would surely be loving and affectionate. So he was ill. He didn't have to be *really* ill because his mother was fifty miles away. A letter would do. So the letter was sent and in due course had precisely the intended effect.

In talking about the need for approval I might equally use Mark Benny's phrase and say that the child wants to be "one of us," and I have never seen a better picture of a child desperately seeking acceptance and approval than the one he draws. I hope I may be forgiven for a quotation from his book *Low Company*. He has visited Hawkspur Camp, and I am glad to say we have won *his* approval!—" . . . I wanted more than ever to be one of them. Nothing in the world seemed so desirable. Excluded from their society, and conditioned to despise all other company, I came to feel there was something radically wrong with myself, something that must be changed if I were ever to be 'wide.' After some introspection I decided that my fault was a want of spirit; I ought to sing to them, and laugh loudly as they did instead of sitting quietly in a corner hoping I wouldn't be noticed. One night, being awakened by sounds of revelry from the sitting-room, I jumped out of bed on impulse and went into them. A roomful of people checked the glasses on the way to their lips to look round at me, a forlorn little figure in pyjamas, framed in the doorway. I sought desperately for a song, and words I had learnt at school came into my mind. I began to quaver:

> Where the bee sucks, there suck I;
> In the cowslip's bell I lie.
> There I crouch when owls do fly
> When owls do fly,
> When owls do . . . .

There was a surprised silence, followed by an outburst of

laughter. Seeing my tearful disappointment, a woman caught me on her lap and began to make a fuss of me; but it was not the spontaneous approval I wanted. Mother scolded me, and sent me back to bed where I sank through black waters of dejection into frustrate sleep."

Benny was more or less fortunate. He did eventually find out, more or less, how to become "one of them," though he afterwards had to learn again (if he will forgive me for putting it like this) to become "one of us." But the distress and unhappiness he suffered may be equally suffered by any other child in normal society who has "missed the boat" in his attempt to "become one of them." And once he feels that the boat has been missed it is not surprising if he acts on the assumption that a miss is as good as a mile. I very well remember my own feelings when I earned the disapproval of my mother without knowing how or why. I don't remember how old I was, but I was so small that my head was level with the top of the sink at which she was working. I asked her where babies came from. I have forgotten her reply (except that it evaded the truth), but I clearly recall the impression I received that—for some reason I could not understand—I had said something that had been better left unsaid. There was no word of disapproval, just an inflection of the voice, and a deliberate refusal to answer truthfully. I was so disturbed by the reception of this perfectly simple question that I never dared ask it again, and was ultimately enlightened at the age of thirteen by an extremely earnest and well-meaning scoutmaster, who took as his text the simple phrase "It's nasty but necessary." I will not refer to the way in which curiosity increases as the square of its denial. That is another matter. What I am talking of now is the distress and bewilderment caused to an innocent little boy who finds that he does not know how to do the right thing, and can find no key to the problem, no clear picture of how to recognize the forbidden fruit of the tree of knowledge and of evil. In my case it didn't matter very much. I had (and still have, I rejoice to say) the best mother in the world, whose love and devotion were tempered with the saving grace of humour, and whose intuitive understanding of her children was such that a mistake of that kind was no sooner made than mended.

But supposing she had been like Tom Beeley's parents. They seemed determined, both of them, to conceal any feeling of affection at all. His mother was a shadowy figure completely dominated by her husband. Mr. Beeley had made Tom feel from his earliest days that he was altogether good for nothing, and had emphasized his belief with many beatings. Tom had many candid friends who supported his father's belief. At twenty-one, in despair of ever being anything or achieving anything, he attempted suicide. I am not sure whether it was a real attempt, or an effort, like Tod Orange's to secure sympathy. But it resulted in his coming to Hawkspur. One day I told him of my firm conviction that he had it in him to make a success of his life, giving reasons. He didn't at first believe me, his reason being that everyone he had ever known had always told him something quite different. They all seem to have been wrong. At any rate, he was man enough, at twenty-three, to marry the girl his father disapproved of, and, knowing father and what the boy used to be, that is a good deal.

The point I am anxious to make in all this is that the person who establishes a real *rapport* with these maladjusted persons, who is really intimate with them, and can see below the veneer of behaviour to the foundation of emotion, is *convinced* that the affective trends are in the direction of seeking approval—of being "a good boy." What happens so tragically often is that the "friend," too much influenced by the overt behaviour, as well as the criticisms of people who do not know the lad as well as he, decides that his intuitive judgment was faulty, and removes his friendship and approval, holding them out like a carrot before a donkey's nose. In general, that mode of behaviour is useless as a therapy; there are so many tempting vegetables growing at the roadside. What he must do is to back his intuitive judgment all along the line. Give the lad unstinted approval in spite of everything he may say or do, approving him always, even if what he does cannot be approved. That's what the mother does when she faces the court, but, alas! she doesn't keep it up outside. Now we at Hawkspur Camp aim at keeping it up in season and out of season. Our chief aim is to make the boy feel that whatever others may think of him, whatever he may have done—or be doing—we approve of him. We are on his side. It is not easy. As often as not the boy thinks there is a catch in it, and sets out to prove that there is a point somewhere at which we shall react like anyone else. One boy even went to the length of conducting himself in such a way that his fellow-members could tolerate him no longer and got up a petition for his removal. He found that I still approved him. I got the petitioners together and told them that the lad they wanted to kick out was potentially the camp's greatest asset. He had more energy and initiative than the lot of them, and I wasn't going to kick out the camp's most valuable future member because they couldn't manage him.

Do not let it be thought, however, that what I have said means that there is never any disapproval at Hawkspur for anti-social conduct. I am insulting the intelligence of my readers by labouring this point, but it is an error into which so many fall. The point is that we have to learn—and so does the boy for that matter—to distinguish between what a boy is and what he does. The orthodox attitude is, "You have done a bad thing. Therefore you are a bad boy. Therefore I cannot love you any more." Our attitude is rather, "You have done a bad thing. Therefore you are a silly ass, but we love you just the same." At first the boy cannot understand this distinction at all, so it often is necessary to refrain from any disapproval at all in a lad's early days at the camp. Even, if other considerations make it possible, to approve "bad" behaviour, until the fact of our approval is well and truly rammed home. If you can understand this point, you will not be surprised as some of our more superficial visitors might well be, if they hear me blazing away in the best barrack-square manner at some unfortunate youth who has done something to annoy me. It may be that, being human, I have just lost my temper. But if it isn't that, it means that I am talking to someone who has learnt that Wills approves of him, and it doesn't matter how much he blinds, it only means he's sore about what you've *done* so there's no need to be upset!

CHAPTER TWO

The Common Cure

"What he needs is a bit of discipline"
ANY MAGISTRATE

JIM PAYNE was sixteen when we first heard of him, and as no one else would pay the small maintenance fee for which we have to ask, we asked the C.O.S. to pay it. They investigated the case with the thoroughness for which they are renowned and finally expressed the view that he wasn't worth wasting money on. He was a thief, a bully, a ne'er-do-well, a menace to the neighbourhood. His own father was beginning to be frightened of him. He was completely illiterate. After that we wondered whether we ought to have him at all, but someone else offered to pay, so he came. He seemed to be all they said except that they hadn't said enough. They had not referred, for example, to his moods of black depression in which he went about with a desperate, unhappy scowl, and could not bear to be spoken to. They had not mentioned the fact that he seemed to be quite unable to do any work. He had had plenty of "discipline" from his father, and that was why father was beginning to be afraid of him—having reached a reasonable size and weight he was beginning to get his own back.

We tried him in various jobs at the camp, but he simply could not stick at one job for more than an hour at the most.

We tried to teach him to read, but without success. Then our Honorary Secretary, Dr. Franklin, put me in touch with an admirable person, Dr. Helene Frank, a German lady who specialized in the teaching of retarded adults. With her help we were able to get him started, but then only with the greatest difficulty. He disliked having to read out of children's books, so I used to use Joyce's admirable translation of Plato's *Symposium*. But even so there was little improvement in his character as a whole. He still pilfered, he still had violent attacks of temper, he still had fits of depression. He was still unable to stick at a job for more than an hour. We tried everything we could think of to try to arouse his interest. I got him writing stories, but he wouldn't do any more after the first. I sometimes used to see him carving heads out of bits of wood, but he invariably threw them on the fire before they were finished. Dr. Franklin bought plasticine, which he never used. I got a friend who used to teach pottery and clay modelling to try him on that—all to no end, and after nearly two years he seemed little different from when he came to us. Then Dr. Helene Frank suggested that he went to Mr. Segal. Mr. Segal ran a painting school in London. He used the teaching of painting as a therapy for various neuroses. After an hour with Payne, Segal said, "I should like this boy three days a week—I think I can help him." He went three days a week, and after a few weeks Segal said, "Not only is this boy going to be helped in himself by painting; if you can improve his general education I think he may even become a painter." However that may be, in four months' time Jim was a different person. He was a human being. There was a different look in his eye, there was purpose in his movements. Pilfering diminished, temper became rarer, and he became a worker. He would work for hours at monotonous jobs in the carpenter's shop and apparently enjoy it. His conversation was fascinating, because as he had never read anything his ideas were original. He saw everything with the eye of an artist and said, "painting is the only thing that matters, really." He wasn't a "whole" man yet, but we had found the clue and he was on the way. Segal's school closed for the summer. I went away on holiday. A new and (owing to the holidays) "unvetted" member was admitted who persuaded Jim and "Yus" to join him in burgling the local pub.

I went to the Quarter Sessions to "speak for them." The Recorder (I don't know who he was) listened with a cynical smile to my rather prolonged appeal ("Aren't you exceeding your mission, Mr. Wills?") in which I told the court the whole of Jim's story, and said how imperative it was that Jim continue with Segal. And when I had quite finished he said, "What this boy wants is a bit of discipline." "Yes," I said, "the discipline he's learning at our camp, the disciplining of himself, not the discipline of Borstal." But Borstal was what he got. He submitted to it patiently for about a year, then, saying "painting is the only thing that matters to me, really," presented himself at Segal's door, a free man, ready to start again where he left off.

Now Jim never had from us any of that discipline that he was supposed to need. Quite the contrary. I remember one period during which he declined to dress when he got up in the morning. He slept in his birthday suit and on arising in the morning put on a most offensive old raincoat and nothing else. This went on for some weeks and I began to be quite worried about it. In fact, I'd just reached a point when I thought I really must do something, steal the wretched thing by dead of night and burn it or something, when, quite suddenly, he started dressing himself. Dressing himself, moreover, with great care, washing, shaving, and greasing his hair, even putting on a collar and tie each day. If you want me to advance some interesting theory to account for this I must disappoint you. Whatever was the cause of this extraordinary phase it meant something quite important in Jim's development and I've never ceased to be glad I didn't interfere with it. I just mention this—one of Jim's many phases—to show how little we gave him of the "discipline" he was supposed to need. And in spite of that (I, of course, say because of that) he eventually found himself and began to become a rational, purposeful human being, with self-respect and his own discipline. If he had had his "bit of discipline" before he came to us he would have kicked against the pricks from the first day, he would have been punished, punishment would have been followed by resentment, more kicking, more punishment and so on until he emerged a hardened, embittered criminal. But, thanks to his experience at Hawkspur, he was able just to ignore the bit of discipline, and when it was over was ready to start again where he left off.

Consider on the other hand, the case of S—— who never had the privilege of coming to Hawkspur Camp. He was committed to Borstal for larceny or shop-breaking. During fifteen months in Borstal his behaviour was absolutely perfect. Not a single black mark, not a single report, not even for any of the petty offences for which one of the inmate leaders could report him. So although his sentence was "not exceeding three years" the authorities thought he should be released. In four months he was back again. He served a further fifteen months during which he not only avoided evil, but actually got plus marks for taking an interest in the House. So again he was released and in four months was in Wandsworth.

Of course no human agency is perfect and we cannot expect Borstal to have one hundred per cent successes. But here is a youth who is repeatedly sent back for further "bits of discipline" when what he needs more than anything else in the world is an opportunity to learn how to get on without it. On the one hand we have Jim Payne, a wild creature who could never be tamed except by the release of his own inner forces, and on the other S——, who was so well tamed that he was helpless without his tamer—for both the remedy is the same. "They need a bit of discipline."

I should not like it to be thought that I consider discipline necessarily an evil. It is not an evil any more than it is a good. It is just something that is necessary to the orderly conduct of an institution in which a large number of people are living together. It is necessary indeed in almost every phase of human activity, but we are concerned here with its use in the treatment of people who are maladjusted socially. If you have seventy young men in one building with only a limited amount of money to spend on them it is important that, for example, clean socks should be issued and dirty ones handed in for washing at stated periods. Unless orderly arrangements are made for things of this kind the life of the staff is quite intolerable and their task an impossible one. There must be rules for carrying out everyday jobs, and people must keep them. That is discipline. Where I quarrel with the disciplinarian—and my quarrel is a bitter one—is that I resent intensely his assumption that by the meticulous and stern enforcement of these rules, some good accrues to the persons upon whom they are imposed. The only person who gets anything out of it is the person for whose convenience it is made, the administrative official. I am all in favour of discipline as a means. I am all against it as an end. And it is considered so vital and valuable an end that all manner of evils flourish in its pursuit, and much needless and fruitless misery and unhappiness are suffered in its name.

When I was in Borstal my house was visited one day by the Governor during "silent hour" when all the inmates are in their rooms studying or following some useful pursuit. I went round with him to visit a few of the boys. I pushed open a door, and the lad, seeing only me, grinned and leaned back on his stool. The grin vanished from his face when he heard the Governor's voice saying, "Stand up, boy, stand up! Don't you stand up when Mr. Wills comes in?" I will forbear to speak of the impossibility of establishing any real relationship of mutual respect and confidence with a person who feels he has to spring to his feet every time one comes near him. I ask you only to consider the consequences if the lad *hadn't* stood up. He would almost certainly have had to go (if he persisted) into the punishment cells, spending his solitary day pounding stones. Three boys were in fact sent to the cells for mischievously shouting something after an officer who had not the personality to command their respect. They had done no evil; they had not upset the routine for the maintenance of which discipline is necessary. But they had done something which, if it passed unpunished, might affect the capacity of the staff to maintain that discipline. They suffered because "discipline must be maintained." They were punished because of the fear in the minds of the authorities, for some future hypothetical breakdown of the machinery. Fear, of course, is one of the principal unconscious motivators of the disciplinarian. But before I speak of the irrational origins of "discipline" let us consider their rationalization in the reasons given in defence of the hypothesis that "a bit of discipline will do him good." The argument is quite simple. "We want so-and-so to acquire certain good habits. We will therefore compel him to do certain things in a certain way under pain of divers penalties. After a few years of, e.g., being made to clean his teeth every morning and evening, he will acquire the habit and will continue to do so." Any psychologist will tell you that things rarely became habits which have predominantly unpleasant associations. It is possible that the boy compelled to clean his teeth might discover that it is pleasant to have a clean mouth, though it is equally possible that, by associating tooth-cleaning with the more unpleasant aspects of discipline, he may spurn the tooth-brush for the rest of his days. What usually happens, as we all know, is that he says, "Thank God I haven't got to do that any more." Three years of enforced early rising had no effect at all on my love of my pillow, and I cannot think that three years of enforced sexual continence is likely to keep anyone away from prostitutes if he happens to care for that form of sexual indulgence. In short, discipline is likely rather to foster a desire for the things it condemns than to encourage abstinence from them. And it has the further grave defect—so often dwelt on elsewhere that I just mention it in passing—that it inhibits initiative and tends to prevent the development of any reliance on one's own capacities and one's own judgment.

In this matter I speak, like St. Paul, of what I do know,

for there was a time when I was a disciplinarian of the first water. At the age of nineteen I went to the Wallingford Farm Training Colony as a "Brother." On my arrival the superintendent, William Henry Hunt (a great man, now, alas, gone to his fathers), peered at me through his thick glasses and bushy eyebrows and said in his gruff voice, "Are you afraid of boys, Mr. Wills?" I, fresh from boys' club work, said that of course I wasn't. It did not take me long to find I was mistaken, but it took me many years to discover what he meant when he said, "You'll be all right then." He simply meant that if I wasn't frightened of them I wouldn't try to make them frightened of me. In less than a week I was reduced to a state of despairing terror. The overwhelming relief when each day ended was equal only to the sickening fear with which I faced each new one. I could do nothing with my boys—and they could do anything they liked with me. How I endured it for nearly a year, when I asked to be transferred to another home, I do not know. In the new home I turned over a new leaf. I began by saying I would report any boy who broke the rule forbidding the wearing of boots in the dormitory. Fifteen boys were fined the routine 2d. from their few coppers pocket-money. The paste-board slips that appeared in their pay envelopes explaining the absence of 2d. I found stuck on my cubicle door. These I collected with care, and duly returned each to its owner. The procedure was to say politely, "Yours, I believe?" and as the victim took the card from my right hand I delivered a vicious blow to the side of his head with my left. From that time on "Woodbine" (the name by which I had been contemptuously called) was to me as "nose" was to Cyrano. I can see now the terror in the eyes of the youth I cornered after a chase of 300 yards of market garden, and I can still feel my sickening glee when my badly-aimed blow struck his soft neck and made him gulp. Often my blows were returned, once I was mobbed and stoned, but in terror I pursued my chosen way, and discipline was achieved. How sweet then to walk in the rowdy day-room and with one glare produce a solemn hush. What sheer delight on Fridays to issue the linen! This was the apex of my week, and I extracted the last ounce of satisfaction from it. Supper was consumed in silence, prayers which followed in a deeper silence (once during supper a boy tried to carry more mugs than my regulation number, so I knocked him down, cocoa and all, and I read for prayers the passage about "whom the Lord loveth he chasteneth"). Then through the silence I walked to the door, where the clean linen was arranged in rows of neat bundles. Almost in a whisper I called out the first name. Its owner walked to the door, picked up his bundle, deposited the dirty articles one by one, and departed. Then I whispered the next name, and so on till all were done. From the beginning of supper to the end of this issue was an hour of perfect silence.

I give you this sordid piece of autobiography as an illustration of what I mean when I say that fear is at the back of discipline. If, during one of my imposed silences, there was the slightest whisper, I was seized with a dreadful feeling of panic, and it was that panic which resulted in the drastic punishments. Throughout my whole period as a disciplinarian I lived with a background of fear—fear of losing control. This fear amounted almost to a phobia, and I was perpetually seeing, or imagining that I saw, signs that those in my care were losing "respect" for me.

I could not convince myself that I was justified in taking the measures that I did merely in order to make things more convenient for myself, so I had to convince myself that it was "good for the boys to have a bit of discipline." So I believe it is with all disciplinarians. I had the misfortune, when I had achieved a certain degree of emancipation from fear, to watch at her work a woman in charge of a "home" for about thirty epileptic children whose ages ranged from about 8 to about 12. For their emotional development children need love as much as they need food for their physical development. This woman, in the interest of "discipline," went against nature. She repressed all her natural desire to love the children in her care, because "boys need discipline." She insisted on an absolute silence during all meals (and at most other times), and the last day of the week I was there I saw her keep the whole home sitting upright, hands behind backs, in perfect silence for twenty minutes, waiting for their rice pudding. She had no conception of the agony she was causing these restless young animals. She was conscious only of the state of panic she found herself in when someone had dared in defiance of the rule to whisper while eating. The position is much the same in a penal institution, though, of course, with much more justification. A small group of men are charged with the duty of doing something very unpleasant to a much larger group, and it's not surprising if they are frightened of their charges. If they would only admit that discipline exists to prevent damage being done to their skins instead of pretending that it is good for the inmates, I would quarrel with them far less!

"Discipline," then, I maintain (as the word is generally understood), derives largely from a fear of the persons upon whom it is imposed. It arises also, of course, from the satisfaction we derive from having power over our fellow-creatures. There are countless examples of that in literature and in life, though they are generally exaggerated examples. But in my view this element is present even in the ordinary "healthy discipline," and I cannot think that any honest disciplinarian can deny that he gets much pleasure from the exercise of his function. Ordinary discipline, bad as it is, has its apparent successes, but in these it succeeds in spite of itself. It sometimes happens that an individual conceives an admiration or affection for the disciplinarian—what the psychologists call a transference. The transference is brought about by the most illogical and irrational of unconscious causes—it may be that the disciplinarian has an inflection of the voice, a colour of the eyebrows, a gesture, which causes an unconscious association in the mind of the disciplined, with someone he loved once—his mother probably. He then cheerfully becomes a disciple in the real sense, copies his master slavishly, carries out his precepts and, I am sorry to say, follows his examples. I had this experience in my disciplinarian days. But how much more fertile the ground for the formation of the transference when it is not full of the tares of authority!

Among the many definitions of "discipline" in the Oxford dictionary is "System of rules for conduct." The delinquent is a person who has been unable to accept the rules that society imposes. He sees them as a restriction upon his liberty, and the more we try to force them upon him, the more he objects. A criminal might indeed be defined as a person upon whom it is impossible to *impose* a discipline. This doesn't conflict with what I have already said about the need for approval. He *does* want the approval of someone but there may be forces at work compelling him to do things which cause him to be denied it. He is perhaps in the position of the little boy of whom I once heard who said, "I'll be good, but I won't be your good."

The task of those who are attempting to get the offender to fit into his environment is first, to abandon the fruitless attempt to force *our* discipline, our good, upon him. Then to devise a means by which he can formulate a system of his own which is not unacceptable to society. A system of which, since he has discovered it himself he can see the value and by which he wants to live. That is how we conceive discipline at Hawkspur Camp.

CHAPTER THREE

This Freedom

"My dear, it's perfectly dreadful!
They do just whatever they like"
MANY VISITORS

Two worthy ladies were discussing Q Camp. One was a Very Well Known Figure among those who are interested in the treatment of juvenile delinquency. The other was, I believe, trying to interest the Very Well Known Figure in Q Camps. "Q Camps?" said the Very Well Known Figure, with a sniff, "Yes, I know all about *them*. That's the place where the boys are allowed to do just as they like."

How many times have we been condemned in those words! Both by the enlightened, who believe that an atmosphere of anarchy with its consequent insecurity is bad for the adolescent and the delinquent; and by the hearty reactionaries who believe that it is thoroughly bad for anyone (if he belong to the lower orders or the lower age groups) to do anything that he likes doing. With the latter group it is useless to spend any time. They are beyond hope of redemption. But I should like to try to answer the criticism where it comes from the former group, because one hears it so often, and it is so often the result of genuine perplexity and real misunderstanding. Such a one was my friend who took a week-end off from his duties in a Borstal Institution to spend a week-end with us at Hawkspur. He was genuinely interested and a good deal impressed by what he saw. "But, Wills," he said, "there are two or three chaps who seem to do nothing but drift around all day. They'll get into slack habits, just when they should be learning habits of work." This is an easy one to answer, though I did not, I believe, have an opportunity to answer it satisfactorily just then. Just who were the lads my friend had seen slacking? Let us examine them. They were Jim Payne, Edward Gough, and Horace Wade. With Horace Wade we were, I must admit, not very successful. But as he had been in a mental hospital before he came to us, and returned to one after leaving us, I do not think we need feel very guilty about him. He ought never to have been at Hawkspur. But he shared with the other two non-workers of that time (and most of the non-workers since) one important characteristic. His mind was a turmoil of conflict. Edward Gough I shall refer to elsewhere. He did not learn to be idle at Hawkspur, and in so far as he was idle he longed to be otherwise. He had given up jobs himself because he found it impossible to attend to them. He had homosexual inclinations which so filled him with horror that all his psychic energy was used up in the conflict between the demands of society and the cravings of his instincts. He could not "concentrate" on anything. One of the first things I noted about him was his interest in the occult—evidence of a desire to find some magical way out of his perplexities—all other methods having failed him. He did try, very often, to do something, but never was able to "stick it" for long. It might have been possible, under an intensely rigid system of discipline, to force him to work. But if that had been done the chances are that we should have been completely unaware of his problems, until, as would inevitably have happened, he went sick with a nervous breakdown. And anyway, the ordinary discipline of everyday life had been insufficient to keep him at work—he had already had a mild breakdown—so he came to us. We let him "do as he liked" (though he had a pretty rough time at the hands of the Camp Council) and concentrated on causes instead of effects. As a matter of fact, Edward never did work very hard at the camp. But he's been a competent wage-earner for two years now, because by the time he left we had got him a good way towards the resolution of his conflicts.

The same thing applies to Jim. For nearly two years he mooched and slacked, and I confess that I did sometimes get worried about him. But the solution to this case came when we discovered the extremely improbable thing that he, an illiterate, could do well—we discovered that he was a "born" painter. From the day we discovered he could paint, and started him on painting lessons, he never looked back. I do not mean that from that time he worked hard merely at painting—any more than I wish to convey that hitherto he had been quite completely idle. He had done odd bits of jobs, working sporadically and inefficiently. But from the time he became a painter, he worked hard and efficiently at monotonous routine camp jobs, without a murmur of complaint. We let him "do as he liked." Yes. But for over eighteen months of his camp life *he simply did not know what he did like*—and neither did we.

I overheard a very interesting conversation one day between Bods and Tod Orange, who was very fond of Bods. Tod had been throwing stones on the roof of a new building we had been putting up. They were big stones, and

Bods thought this was an activity that should be discouraged. He had taken Tod to task (Oh yes, that does sometimes happen at Hawkspur!) about it, and Tod replied, "You shut your mouth—I shall do what I bloody well like." "That's right," said Bods, "that's what I want you to do. I want you to do what you like. But you don't like smashing things up. You're doing that because you think Dick'll be impressed by it. But you don't *like* it at all." And Tod burst into tears. Bods had hit the nail right on the head. People who are free to do anything do not necessarily do what they *like.* Our whole aim at Hawkspur is to get the lads to do what they like, but unhappily there are all manner of influences and compulsions at work making them do things they do not like. Let me give you the history of Roland Leaf. He was a pleasant, attractive lad of 22 or so, who had been brought up in a nautical school under a very rigid system of discipline. Our account of his early adolescence is incomplete, but at any rate by the time he was twenty-one he had served two or three short sentences for offences in connection with motor cars. He came to us (though we did not normally accept ex-prisoners) after serving a sentence of, I think, three months. He came from prison to "this place where they do as they like." What did Roland Leaf like? He liked to be popular, he liked to be respected, he liked to be admired, he liked above all to be loved. We tried, so far as we were able, to supply his needs, but the need for affection was so great as to be pathological, and we could not meet it. He used to come down to the cottage my wife and I had at that time in the village, and help us with distempering and wall-papering, at which he claimed to be expert. In the process he soon made the acquaintance of various of our neighbours in the village.

His manner with women was irresistible. He was very soon "at home" in the bungalow of a middle-aged lady who, knowing something about him, was anxious to help him. He gave her dancing lessons. When he told her he was an authority on antiques, she believed him. "'You could tell by the way he handled it that he knew all about these things." "It" being a perfectly valueless pot which Roland said he could sell for a considerable sum—if only he had his fare to the nearest town. "What a lovely home you have, Florence," he said to a young widow. "How lovely it is to sit in this corner by the fire and feel that this is home! I never had a home," and shortly afterwards borrowed the money she had painfully saved for her rent. He was neither wicked nor insincere. He was just driven to these things by an inexplicable compulsion. Inexplicable, that is, to him and to me. But probably not inexplicable, after a time, to a competent medical psychologist. So as it was obvious that he was going to get into trouble, and as we could not hope to deal with him without the aid of a psychotherapist, we made plans. We arranged for him to go to London, to live in a hostel for a few months while he had intensive psychotherapy. Then, when he was beginning under treatment to make a little progress, he was to return to the camp. But this was one of those well-laid schemes of mice and men. Roland took one look at the hostel and walked out of it, having expressed his opinion to the warden in a few well-chosen but unprintable words. He came back to the camp. I was firm. "What'll you have," I said, "the arrangements we have made for you, or home?" "Home," said Roland, calling, as he probably thought, my bluff. But I wasn't bluffing. I couldn't accept the responsibility of housing a person like that—the camp had a bad enough name already. So I gave him his fare and put him on the bus. His home was two hundred miles away, but within a fortnight he was back in the village again. As the camp was closed to him, a very fine woman in the village put him up, in the hope of being able to make something of him. But her good will exceeded her wisdom. Before long he had made the village too hot to hold him, and cleared off on a borrowed motor-bike. He had come back to our village, I am convinced (from my knowledge of him), not because he thought they were a lot of "suckers" upon whom he could prey, but because there were people there who were genuinely fond of him. But he could not resist his curious compulsions. He could not do as he liked! He did not steal the motor-bike. It belonged to someone he knew quite well, and when its usefulness was finished he put it in a garage and sent a card to its owner!

A few weeks later he was before the bench in a West of England town on no less than twenty-one charges, most of them connected with motor-cars. They treated him (considering his record) leniently, and gave him only six months. He was a model prisoner, earned his full remission and in due course came out. He stepped almost straight into a car, ditched it when the petrol was exhausted and, in a succession of stolen cars, travelled across country to the camp. He arrived about three o'clock in the morning in a handsome Vauxhall. Fetched out of my bed at that hour I could not pretend to be pleased to see him, especially in what I felt sure was a stolen car. I spoke to him as affably as I could, but did not offer him a bed. So he drove off, and early that morning gave himself up at a neighbouring police station, saying he couldn't stand it any longer. Once again, by a curious coincidence, there were twenty-one charges, but this time he was arraigned at Quarter Sessions. Asked if he had anything to say before sentence was passed, Roland said, "Yes, sir. Please will you send me to Penal Servitude?" The Recorder, before delivering sentence, dwelt on the "orgy of crime" in which this youth had indulged, and the leniency with which he had hitherto been treated. Then he went on to say that this was one of those cases in which the wishes of the prisoner should be met. "Not, however, because they are the wishes of the prisoner, but because the occasion demands it. Three years' Penal Servitude." So Roland got his own way, and now he's doing what he likes in a convict prison. Yes. Doing what he likes. I said earlier on that he liked to be popular, he liked to be respected, admired, loved. The way to achieve those ends is to toe the line, adhere to the mores of the society in which you find yourself. At the camp he tried desperately hard to do that, but it was beyond him. He wrote to his sponsor that he had never been so miserable in his life. The freedom was too much for him. Every morning without fail he had to go to all the trouble of deciding for himself whether or not he would get out of bed. Every day *he* had to make the decision for himself, whether or not he should do any work, and every day and all day it was he that had to apply the compulsion to keep Roland at it. He was not used to it. It was too much for him. But in prison! His feeling towards prison was like that of Rupert Brooke for Grantchester . . "There's peace, and holy quiet there." There, while he was not able to secure the love he craved, it was perfectly simple to secure those other things he liked—respect, approbation, and the rest of them. In prison it is much, much easier to toe the line than not. Never, there, was he called upon to make any of these difficult choices, and the responsibility for keeping Roland at work rested with anyone except Roland. So in prison he was happy, and to prison he continually returned.

I have told Roland's story at some length, and it might appear that in doing so I have spoiled my own case. Here was a man who was, on my own confession, positively *driven* to prison by the lack of authority and discipline at Hawkspur Camp. But it was not only the freedom of Hawkspur Camp that was too much for him. The freedom of ordinary society was also far too much for him. And Hawkspur was not intended for such as he. We tried him, in our early days, as an experiment—it was difficult to see what would happen to him if we did not—but we never made the same mistake again. Hawkspur was intended for beginners in delinquency, not for hardened cases. But Roland was different only in degree, and not in kind, from our other members. For them, too, the freedom of ordinary society is too much. What is the remedy? Put them somewhere where there is even less freedom than in ordinary society? I think not. I am sure the only remedy is to increase the amount of their freedom for a spell so that, by learning to control themselves in this greater freedom, the relatively less free atmosphere of normal society will present fewer problems to them. The fact that I refused to keep Roland Leaf does not mean that I would prescribe a different treatment for persons of his type. But for him, I think his dose of freedom should be applied in an environment quite cut off from ordinary society, so that society is protected from him during the period of treatment. And, of course, as I have said, the freedom is not of itself a sufficient treatment—it must be allied with psychotherapy.

This Freedom

When we first started the camp I thought in my innocence that in this free-and-easy, do-as-you-like atmosphere, everyone would be perfectly happy. I should have known better. Of course they're not, and there are two principal reasons for this. One is that most of the chaps who come to the camp are profoundly dissatisfied with themselves. Society has made them feel that they are useless—and worse. In the main they want, like most of us, to be thought well of. They have failed, they are disappointed, and they hate themselves. How easy —and how usual—to transfer this hatred (or to displace it, as the psychologists say) to one's environment. We all know the "disappointed man" who grouses about everything. At Hawkspur we have disappointed youths—and they grouse about the camp. We are continually seeing examples of this. Tom Beeley, since you have met him elsewhere, is as good an example as any. Poor Tom was just one mass of guilt-feeling and shame. He had been hectored and bullied all his life over trifles, and now he had brought shame upon his respectable family by appearing in the police court. Observe Tom's reactions to the camp. Immediately on arrival he said what a wonderful place it was. Being intensely interested in other people's opinions of him he was a bit of a dandy, and therefore formed a mental picture of himself in the appropriate kit for helping with the excavating we were doing just then. He even spoke some of it aloud—"I shall be able to wear an open-necked shirt here." So he tried to win our approval by saying how nice "our place" was. But of course that lasted only a few days. The person whose good opinion Tom was really anxious to win was his own. He hated himself, so he gradually shifted that hatred onto his surroundings. He became our prize grouser. At first furtively and later, when he found that he could do so without being made to suffer for it, openly. He painted in large letters across his bunk "The legion of the lost." (Dear, dear, what lack of discipline, said some of the visitors to each other.)

Tom was having psychotherapy from a medical psychologist in London, and presently it came to my ears that on his weekly visits he was taking the opportunity to tell the doctor dreadful tales about the horrors of life at Hawkspur Camp. The doctor asked him if he had been to me with his complaints. He had to confess that he had not. He knew that many of his complaints were groundless; that where they were not groundless the remedy lay as much with him as with me, and perhaps most important of all he had a sneaking feeling that if he had all the things he complained of rectified, it would be much more difficult for him to find something to grouse about—and he did *so* need something to grouse about. But eventually, after a good deal of prodding, he sought an interview with me in order to lodge his complaints.

Alas! I cannot remember what all his grouses were. With regard to the first half-dozen or so I was able to say, "Why come to me with these complaints? These are things of common concern, and any action that needs to be taken should properly be taken by the Camp Council. See the Secretary of the Camp Council and have them put on the agenda for the next meeting." "Pooh," he said, "Camp Council!—what's the good of that? Camp Council's no good. It never does anything—its sheer waste of time going to it." This was a common criticism of the Camp Council. What it really meant was, "If I go with this to the Camp Council we shall all agree upon something and it will be as much my responsibility as anyone else's to see that that something is carried out. But I would rather be *made* to carry it out by someone in authority." This was very true of Tom. Apart from his present grouses he was always complaining in general about the lack of discipline, but was highly indignant when it was suggested that real discipline would involve punishing him for divers offences. But that by the way. Tom's first half-dozen complaints cut no ice with me, and they were never brought before the Camp Council, so far as I remember. But then he produced something which he thought would floor me. He said the latrines were filthy and insanitary. It was no good, he said, going to Camp Council with that, because the only real solution was a different type of latrine bucket, and that was not in the province of the Camp Council (which had no funds in those early days). I told him that neither in using nor in taking my turn at emptying the latrines had I noticed that they were filthy and insanitary. But it was still, I said, a matter for the Camp Council. If Camp Council agreed with him that a different type of bucket was needed instead of the five-gallon oil drums we were then using, it could send a recommendation to the Q Camps Committee in London, where it would be very carefully considered. "Huh," says Thomas, "we all know what *that* means." I was going to dispute that point with him. Camp Council had never yet sent a recommendation to the Q Camps Committee so he couldn't possibly know what that meant. But he had another poser for me. "All the chaps," he said, "hate sleeping between blankets. Why can't we have sheets?" I said that it was very funny that "all the chaps" had never mentioned to me their reluctance to sleep between blankets. Perhaps they knew that I also slept between blankets and that therefore they wouldn't get much change out of me. After all, it was a camp, and not the Savoy Hotel. And why didn't they try asking for them? Again the contemptuous snort. But I kept him to it, and reluctant though he was I made him raise these two points, at least, at Camp Council. Actually, I don't think many of the fellows cared tuppence whether they had sheets or not. But Tom, once he was committed to it, did a good deal of lobbying, and they thought it might be good fun to back him up and see if they could make me look silly. So in due course a recommendation went from the Camp Council to the Q Camps Committee that proper latrine buckets be provided, and that there be sheets for the beds. These requests *were* very carefully considered by the Committee, and the sheets and buckets were provided. This was of course a great triumph for Thomas Beeley. But did it stop his grousing? it certainly did not. But it did help him, just a little bit, towards the realization that it was really Tom and not Hawkspur Camp that he was dissatisfied with.

But what is all this, you may ask, to do with boys doing as they like? It has a great deal to do with it. Protagonists of the "give him a bit of discipline" school argue that discipline (orthodox brand) gives a chap time for reflection, makes him think a bit, makes him face up to things, and so forth. It may give him the opportunity for all these things, but what it dismally fails to provide is the stimulus. Only freedom can do that, and the process is not a painless one. Those who believe in "making it hot" for the offender think they can do so by means of a rigid discipline. They would be surprised if they knew how many there are like Roland Leaf who simply love it. They will be even more surprised, and, I fear incredulous, when I tell them that by *avoiding* discipline of the authoritarian type we can make it much "hotter" for them—though that is of course a by-product, and not our aim. Under a system of rigid discipline Tom would simply have groused as he did at Hawkspur (though with better cause), and would never have had the opportunity which our freedom gave him of beginning to learn that the fault, dear Brutus, is not in our stars but in ourselves, that we are unhappy.

But it's after the grousing stage has passed its peak, and they are beginning to acquire a little self-respect (and therefore need to grouse less), that things begin to get really "hot" for them.

I said a little earlier on that two things contribute to the discomfort of the campers. One is that they come to us hating themselves, and displace their hatred onto the camp. The other is the very fact of being free, of having to discipline one's self, instead of being disciplined by others is a burden, as Roland Leaf found it, though he, as I have said, was an extreme case. So we have to temper the wind to the shorn lamb by providing just as much discipline as they need —and they create it themselves through the medium of the Camp Council. So now we see self-government in a new light. It is not merely a privilege that is bestowed upon them because we superior mortals think the experience might be useful for them. It is an absolute necessity to enable them to set a term to the horrors of personal self-discipline which we have thrust upon them by refusing to be authoritarian. And as *they* control the machinery they can roughly suit it to their needs. Thus we have the man who is notoriously the untidiest, himself suggesting that there be a fine of one penny for untidy bunks.

But there is still more than all that in this freedom. Probably the most important aspect is one upon which I have not yet touched.

The youths who come to Hawkspur Camp are in some sense disordered. They are not whole. When I say they are not whole I do not mean they are not all there. I do not mean their minds are deranged (though we have had some of those). I mean that they are—if you like—socially sick. More accurately, they are emotionally deranged or disordered. In so far as they are sick, we have to get as complete a clinical picture as possible in order to know how to set about the cure. We get to know as much about their past history as we can. But the amount we are able to get is limited, and not always reliable. We must therefore rely in a large measure upon our own observation of the symptoms. What would *you* think of a doctor who tried to blind himself to the symptoms of his patient and then had the temerity to say that as he could see no symptoms there was was nothing wrong with the patient? That is what we should be doing if we were to subject our members to an imposed discipline. By making it impossible for them to diverge from a certain pattern of behaviour we should make it impossible to see when and where, and with how much force, they would diverge under normal circumstances. It is possible for a person under discipline never to display a single symptom, and go out into the world again 'quite untouched. But in the freedom of Hawkspur we see them as they really *are*. Very often the symptom complained of in the lad's history does not show itself even at Hawkspur, where we usually bring out the worst in everybody, but others, usually more revealing, take their place. We must never lose sight of the fact that the delinquency is not in itself the thing we are out to cure. The delinquency is only the symptom, and when the "disease" is cured, the symptom will disappear.

Let us take a few examples of boys who were sent to us with apparently the same symptom but in whom, in the freedom of the camp, totally different "diseases" were discovered and treated.

"Slosher" Hare stole from cigarette machines; Charley Horsfall stole from his employer; Hans Schmidt stole from his schoolfellows. All had the same outstanding symptom, and if we had known no more about them than that—how little should we have known. Actually we did know, even when they first came, a little more about them than that—we knew something of their backgrounds. Slosher had been brought up in a "home." Charley came from a highly respectable, religious, lower middle-class family with a nice house in the suburbs of a provincial town. Hans was a German Jew, whose mother was the widow of an impecunious professor. Well-meaning friends had brought him over from Hitler's Germany and sent him to a well-known public school.

We watched them.

If he had had to stand to attention, or say "sir" every time he spoke to me, I should never have known that Hans was wearing a mask. Everyone who stands to attention wears a mask. Everyone who speaks to a "superior" wears a mask. But masks at Hawkspur are unusual. Hans had been dreadfully hurt, and was ashamed to show any sign of it. At sixteen he was, apparently, cold, sophisticated, and unapproachable. But you can't keep that up for long at Hawkspur, and when he found that I could talk to him about his misdemeanours with no hint of condemnation he began to thaw.

We continued to watch.

We found him showing off. We found him at all points trying to show his superiority to other members of the camp. What, under "discipline," do you do with the swanker? You take him down a peg. Not so us—we did all we could to give him something to swank about. This showing off helped us to interpret his background, and confirmed our suspicions. Tall, well built, handsome, he had been in Germany an object of contempt and worse because of his race. Then he came to England and lived among a lot of young gentlemen whose chief criterion of excellence seemed to be the amount of money a fellow could throw about. He had practically none. His crushed ego was crying out for approbation, after his experiences in Germany, and now it could be acquired by means of money. So he got the money. Then he was discovered and the last state was worse than the first. He sank to the depths of misery and shame, and was hurt so cruelly that he had to wear a mask to hide his pain and shame. All his efforts to secure approbation had brought him only lower than ever, but with a little sympathy he was ready to start again—one is pretty resilient at sixteen. Once he was ready to start again we had to put in his way opportunities for restoring his self-respect. As they came along, he took them with avidity. It worked. He has never looked back since. But we were only able to discover so much about him because we had no artificial barriers separating us. He "did as he liked," and we were able to get to know him.

Charley Horsfall and Slosher Hare were contemporaries at the camp—Hans had been much earlier. But like Hans they had both been pilferers—and we watched them, too. Hans never stole anything all the time he was with us, but Charley and Slosher did. Slosher, brought up in an orphanage, stole exotic ties and shirts from Adrian. Charley pilfered money all over the place, *and always took pains to be found out.* Slosher was a dreadful little bully. Charley, ten years older and nearly twice as big, was his chief victim. Slosher then was probably passing on what he had earlier received. A little enquiry proved this to be true—a bullying father, a mother no better than she should be, before he went to the "home." He had never been loved, and his stealing was probably the symbolical stealing of affection. A rough-and-ready diagnosis? Perhaps so. But one for which the appropriate medicine can never do anyone any harm. We gave it to Slosher, and it cured him.

Charley was a tougher nut to crack. He always saw to it, by some silly mistake or unconscious slip, that his pilferings were discovered. He took merciless beatings from little Slosher without a murmur. He was anxious to become an evangelist. What did all these symptoms point to? They pointed to a tremendous accretion of guilt feelings, crying out for punishment. He wanted to be an evangelist because he had identified himself with all the sinners who need to be saved—a very frequent kind of mental somersault. His silly mistakes leading to his thefts being discovered betokened a wish for punishment. But we never gave it to him. On the contrary I, a Quaker and a pacifist, even encouraged him to hit back when Slosher sloshed him. I even went so far as to encourage him to use bad language. Why? Because although I am not an authoritarian I did represent Authority to Charley. And Authority told him there's nothing to feel guilty about in sticking up for yourself; there's nothing very frightful, meriting eternal damnation, in using a few cuss words.

Authority even went so far as to give him the money he stole from time to time, so that he could replace it before it could be discovered, and Authority—from whom he first got his ideas about guilt— (though Authority then spoke through other lips) was now telling him that he really did not deserve all that punishment. All that, I admit, was mere scratching at the surface, and we needed also the help of the psychotherapist. But gradually—oh, very gradually—we were able to undermine the idea that Charley was a sinful creature who must continually seek punishment. When he began to use bad language freely, and with a sense of enjoyment, we were positively pleased, because it meant that he was no longer piling up future punishments for himself every time he committed some trifling offence.

It had been Charley's practice to procure punishment for himself by getting himself sacked from his jobs. He's been holding one down for nearly two years now, so we hope the trick is done.

Now—here were three pilferers. Three youths whose manifest symptom was the same. But they had three totally different "diseases." Only by watching for their other symptoms in an atmosphere in which they were quite free to display them could we find those other symptoms, relate them to what we knew of their history, make a diagnosis, and effect a cure.

CHAPTER FOUR

Camp Council

"They say, '*Why* can't fellows be allowed to do what they like, when they like and *as* they like . . .'"

THE WIND IN THE WILLOWS

"CARRIED ANONYMOUSLY," said the Chairman (aged 17), and it was agreed, with acclamation, that Tom should pay Harry five Woodbines for the hire of his Wellingtons, which Tom had borrowed without permission.

In many another Institution I know—in almost any other, in fact—Tom, being the bigger, would just have borrowed the Wellingtons and that would have been that. Or if Harry had tried to do something about it he could only have done so by reporting the matter to someone, which would bring him into contempt, even among those whose job it is to maintain "discipline," as a sneak. Tom would be given a lecture and told not to do it again, with the result that the next time he wanted them he would say to Harry, "Lend me your Wellingtons or——" And Harry would receive a longer lecture for sneaking. It is, of course, nothing but nonsense to talk about "the schoolboy code" in connection with sneaking. The opprobrium with which the sneak is regarded was created and is maintained by teachers and officials. It is part of the hocus-pocus of "discipline" that those in authority are slightly holy, and can do no wrong.

The sneak not only reveals an imperfection in the System and hence by implication in those who are running it. He also calls for some action on the part of the authority, which is very annoying because the object of the System is to minister to the convenience of the authority, and not to make him get up out of his chair at inconvenient moments. So Authority has no use for sneaks, and as quite obviously the sneakee hasn't either, how simple to blame it all on the "schoolboy code." So, if Harry and Tom had been elsewhere, they would both have been made to feel guilty, and Harry would have gone about in fear of a surreptitious smack on the nose for sneaking. At Hawkspur the position is very different. Harry's Wellingtons are missing. He sees Tom coming back from the village with them on, challenges him, and, getting no satisfaction, says he's going to "bring it up" at the Camp Council. On Thursday morning the Secretary of the Camp Council says "Anything for the Agenda?" and Harry says, "Yes, I want to bring up about Tom pinching my Wellingtons." So it is duly entered on the Agenda—"Charge—Harry *v.* Tom—wearing Harry's Wellingtons, without permission." The matter is discussed at some length, evidence is brought, and everyone sees the justice of a little compensation in a case like this, though the Duke (that's me), with characteristic perversity, takes the side of the chap who borrowed them rather than the aggrieved party. Perhaps the discussion gets rather heated, but that's all to the good, because the steam is all blown off instead of being pent up with danger of an explosion later on. By the time the matter is finished it is being discussed even with a measure of hilarity. Tom feels that the award of five fags damages is probably quite fair because even his own friends vote for it.

And so the matter is amicably settled, and Harry has no fear of a smack on the nose for sneaking, partly because there's no such thing as sneaking at Hawkspur, and partly because the Camp Council doesn't allow bullying—of which more later.

That is the procedure at the present moment, so far as the judicial function of the Camp Council is concerned. But there is no hard-and-fast immutable system about our self-government. In fact we don't call it self-government, because so many people seem to think that self-government means giving the inmates (we call them members) the whole responsibility for running things which they can only imperfectly understand. Of course, it doesn't mean that. The sphere of the Camp Council's authority is a limited one—it is limited to the domestic affairs of the camp, and is concerned primarily with people's relations to one another, and the day-to-day conduct of family life. Further, the Council consists not only of members. As we all live together, we all have a voice in the affairs of government. So we have adopted Dr. Franklin's happy phrase—"shared responsibility." The members share with the staff the job of running the camp and the staff accept the jurisdiction of the Camp Council on those matters with which the Council is concerned.

When I was in America I had the privilege of visiting an institution for young offenders which was known as a Junior Republic. It was a splendid affair. They had their President, Vice-President, Cabinet, Comptroller, Judge, Attorney-General, lawyers, policemen and all the paraphernalia of American Democracy including a gaol, though I believe the gaol has since been done away with. Although in spite of all this elaborate machinery for self-government the Director found it necessary to administer at least one good hiding with his own fists during my week-end there, I have no doubt that it all helped the boys to understand their function as citizens when they returned to normal society. But I quarrel with all that because it is such a slavish imitation of what is, after all, not necessarily an ideal system of government. It shows how a certain "system of rules for conduct" works. It does less, I think, to show why it is so necessary to have such a system at all. On the other hand, there was the interesting experiment run by Mr. Russell Hoare some twenty-five years ago—Riverside Village, in Lincolnshire. I believe, incidentally, that Mr. Hoare now holds very different views on the question of authority and discipline, as he has joined a Roman Catholic order. But at Riverside, so far from having any system of government, Mr. Hoare insisted that the children should all do exactly what seemed good to them, and considered it quite wrong for the staff to attempt to influence them, except purely by example. In an address which he gave to the Friends' Guild of Teachers, Mr. Hoare criticized Homer Lane's Little Commonwealth on much the same grounds as I have criticized the Junior Republic, though I think with less justification, and said "I am not out to make good little citizens. I am out to make rebels." (I quote from memory as I have mislaid the paper which Mr. Hoare kindly gave me some years ago.)

I think it is something of that sort that we are trying to do at Hawkspur Camp. I do not mean that we are trying to make everyone "agin the government." I mean that our aim is to develop the capacity for personal judgment so that when he goes from us the lad does not necessarily accept the standards of the first group with which he happens to come into contact, even if that group happen to be a group of normal citizens. Criticism is the dynamic of democracy, and if its citizens have lost that capacity, we had much better have a dictatorship, which will at any rate be efficient. So we don't foist a system on them and say, "Here's a system—work it." So far as we have a system at all it has been built up very gradually, with much squabbling, and very often we rub it out altogether and start all over again. I say to newcomers, "This is how we do things at present. If you don't like it, try to change it—you only have to get the majority to agree with you." For we haven't, I am sorry to say, found yet any better system than counting noses as a basis of government. We do sometimes distinguish between a "law" and an "agreement." Someone will say, e.g., "What's the good of making a law if some people don't keep it?" (for we have very few penalties), and then we try to get everyone to *agree* to the suggestion under discussion. This is the beginning of the acceptance of mutual obligation, and is of course much better than making "laws." Our day-room is an old Army hut heated by a slow-combustion stove. Across one side of the stove is a home-made settee with flat cushions along the seat. Some members developed the habit of removing these cushions to sit on at meal-times, and often they weren't put back. I initiated an agitation against this practice and after a prolonged discussion no law was made forbidding it, but we *agreed* not to do it. With one exception. One young man didn't see why he should not continue to use the cushion in this way, so he refused to agree. The agreement was solemnly entered in the minute book, the exception being mentioned by name. For some time the exception conscientiously removed the cushion before each meal, folded it, and sat on it. But public opinion became too much for him after a time, and the practice stopped altogether.

That is by the way. I was saying that we tell them when they come that if they don't like our way of doing things it is up to them to get them altered. And very often they are altered. We even had a period during which the system of government was anarchic. It is a longish story, but not without interest. For some time the Camp Council had not been functioning effectively. Rules and agreements were made, but not carried out, with the result that essential work was left undone. Latrines were not emptied, day-room and bunk-houses were dirty and untidy, meals were late or even not prepared at all, and so on. I would have been prepared to let this state of affairs continue until the members themselves did something about it if I had had no one to consider but myself and the people at the camp. But we have to satisfy public health authorities, and we have people visiting the camp with a view to sending members or giving us money who, while they may be fairly sympathetic, only think that a system of self-government is working if everything is running smoothly. So I issued a ukase. I put up a notice to the effect that pocket-money (which had hitherto been two shillings per head irrespective of whether any work had been done) would in future be variable according to the amount of work done. I said I didn't like to be a dictator, but if an inspector came and found the camp in a filthy mess, it would be I who got it in the neck, and not they. The notice was put up at tea-time. It seemed to be taken quietly, and I heard no comment. The next morning I was on kitchen duty. (The system about kitchen was then, as now, that everyone takes a turn, two people each day). After breakfast I began to hear sounds of intense activity—hammering and so on—coming from one of the bunk-houses. About eleven o'clock a piece of paper was thrown out of one of the bunk-house windows, containing an ultimatum. About half the camp had barricaded themselves in the bunk-house, and said they proposed to stay there until my "new scheme" was revoked. I was delighted to see this sign of life after so many weeks of inertia, and I made plans to have their food sent over at dinner-time. Unfortunately, however, they all crept out about five to one and came across for something to eat. In due course the whole thing was discussed. I said I didn't want to interfere with the functions of the Camp Council, but if their failure to carry out their function meant that I and the reputation of the camp had to suffer I had to do something to protect myself. I said I didn't mind what they did or how they did it so long as at least the essential services were carried out. One of them said he could devise a system of government far better and more effective than the one that had failed now, or the footling thing that I was attempting to impose on them, if only the staff wouldn't poke their noses in. I argued that we had to live there as well as they, but said even so we would be glad to agree to the members alone being constituted a sub-committee to formulate a constitution. It was to be done by a given date and in the meantime I would withdraw my objectionable plan. (A year or so later a very similar plan was voluntarily adopted.) The time arrived for the presentation of the plan but it wasn't ready. There was an acrimonious discussion in the course of which the member who had said they could evolve something gave vent to the apophthegm that the only difference between the staff and the members was that the staff thought they were bloody perfect, but the members knew *they* weren't. So it was postponed a week. At the next meeting the "constitution" that was brought forward was a proposition that anarchy was the ideal form of government, and should be put into effect. Carried by a large majority. I said anarchy was O.K. by me provided it cooked the dinner and emptied the latrines, but kept to myself the prediction that they would soon find no rules a greater tyranny than having a few. It took them about a month to learn that. Then one of the members (while I was away for a week-end) called a meeting of all those who were fed up with anarchy, with a view to re-introducing law and order. Somewhat more than half the members attended it, while the Anarchists rallied their troops for an attack on the meeting-place, in the course of which they smashed one window but inflicted no casualties upon the Constitutionalists. The meeting was held in my office, but whether the words "Wills is a one" were written by Anarchists or Constitutionalists I have never yet learned. However, the result of this meeting was that the Camp Council was re-convened and law and order re-established, in spite of the rather frightening record in the minutes of how "opposing members, calling themselves the rebels, . . . on leaving, said, 'All right, you have the majority, but we will smash every proposal you make.' "

I was interested to read in one of Mr. A. S. Neill's books that he had a somewhat similar experience at Summerhill, with apparently the same incidental sequel, namely, that although everybody was heartily glad when "anarchy" came to an end, the pro-anarchists still look back upon it as a sort of golden age when everybody did everything he should and everything went smoothly. I suspect that this is because, while everybody disliked the discomfort and disorganization of anarchy, they all loved the feeling (due to a complete misconception of the true meaning of the word) that they no longer had the responsibility of anything at all, and could sit back and watch things slide with no accretion of guilt feeling. For one of the greatest difficulties about self-government is that in the main people do not care to accept responsibility unless they are very well rewarded.

But "'twas a famous victory." I do not mean by that that the restitution of orthodoxy was a victory. I mean the discovery by practical experience that if people living together are to enjoy the amenities of a civilized existence, certain responsibilities must be shouldered by somebody. They had too much savvy to hand the responsibility and its concomitant authority to one person—so they shared it between them. We did then have something approaching a "golden age," but only, I am happy to say, for a few weeks. If things go with clockwork regularity for long I become worried—education is really only taking place when things are not going too smoothly. I have driven in my time a long series of "old crocks" of cars with the result that urgent necessity has forced upon me at any rate a nodding acquaintance with the principles of the internal combustion engine, which I should never have acquired if I had always been driven about in a chauffeur-driven Rolls Royce. Most of us these days have been carried along in a social system which was made by our fathers and administered by someone other than ourselves. Some of us need the experience of driving an old crock to find out how the machine really works. I never tire of quoting Browning on this point—

The Hawkspur Experiment

"For thence,—a paradox
Which comforts while it mocks—
Shall life succeed in that it seems to fail."

I have quoted that to generation after generation of Hawkspurians when they have become depressed about the apparent inadequacy and futility of our shared responsibility. I have even had to quote it quite often to my colleagues, though anyone who is really quite incapable of grasping it is no use as a staff member at Hawkspur Camp.

This business of unwillingness to accept responsibility may have more in it than meets the eye, and it is not only the obviously irresponsible who need to learn the lesson.

One day I was presented with a petition to be sent to the Q Camps Committee, which had been organized by some of the more responsible members of the camp.

"We, the undersigned, believe that T. Miner is a menace to the camp. He destroys everything we try to do, and we therefore ask the London Committee to remove him from the Camp." Here followed the names of nearly every member of the camp, and the Petition was duly forwarded to the Q Camps Committee in London.

We were all very heartily sick of T. Miner, and not without reason. He did, at this time, very little work himself, and delighted in destroying what others had done. Feeling against him had been growing for some time, and reached its culmination one night when, returning from a party in the Camp Chief's quarters (which Miner had refused to attend), we found the day-room furniture piled in a heap, a number of duckboards which had just been made as part of our campaign against the mud knocked to pieces, and the concrete pillars in which a new building was to rest torn out of the ground. T. Miner had a dominating personality and usually managed to win or coerce acquiescence in his misdemeanours; but this time he had gone too far.

Although the petition was addressed to the "London Committee," I naturally as their representative had to discuss it with the petitioners. We had many discussions, some of them acrimonious. One of the things I said was that I didn't see why we should be called upon to chuck T. Miner out at the request of the members, when they had never attempted to do anything about him themselves. "We're trying to do something about him now," they said. "No, you're not," I replied. "Often Tom has done this sort of thing before and you haven't even complained. Some of you have even helped him. Now, as a result of your neglect of his lesser offences he has gone a bit too far even for you, and what do you do? You try to shove it onto the London Committee. You're shirking your responsibilities." And that has been one of the outstanding characteristics of our Camp Council—they never *wanted* the responsibility of running their own affairs. Both as a community and as individuals they have much preferred that someone should give orders which they were expected to obey. I have considered it one of my chief functions to get them to see how necessary it is that they should accept the responsibility for their own behaviour. And the Camp Council is just one of the means to that end.

Your ordinary schoolmaster or Borstal official is delighted when he finds his boys "amenable to discipline." I, on the other hand, consider amenability to discipline one of the greatest evils I have to cure. The Germans, taking them by and large, are a race of people amenable to discipline. That's why they've got Hitler. If we do not want an English Hitler —if we want to keep alive that flame of freedom which flickers across the pages of our history—however feebly at times—from the time of the Witenagemote, we must see to it that our people are not "amenable to discipline." S——, whom I spoke of in Chapter Two, was amenable to discipline, and that is why he could not keep out of Borstal.

Do not let it be thought, however, that only the docile and obedient need to learn to create their own discipline instead of merely accepting any that is imposed on them. There is a sense in which even the most fractious person may be said to have accepted an imposed discipline. If a lad is forever kicking over the traces it might be said that surely *he* needs a "bit of discipline." Not at all. The "amenable" shirks responsibility because authority shoulders it for him. So with the "unamenable"—perhaps not always, but very often. He argues, "Authority has taken on the job of ordering my conduct. Very good, that means I don't have to bother about it. I can do just whatever I please. If Authority happens to approve of it, all well and good. If Authority disapproves, I shall be made to pay for it, so that account is squared. So I can do as I like." My old schoolmaster frankly used to encourage this attitude. "Please do not think," he said to me in a pained voice when I had been caught in the act of arranging an ingenious booby trap of pins and pen-nibs for the discomfort of the boy in front, "Please do not think I have any wish to interfere with your little pleasures. By no means. I want you to enjoy yourself to the full. But, of course, we all have to pay for our pleasures in this world, and even you, my dear Wills, are not exempt. Hold out your hand." So the "unamenable" thinks he has a perfect right to steal, laze, or bully so long as he "takes what's coming to him." The effect of being brought up on this doctrine is sometimes very serious, producing a pathological state in which the victim is perpetually seeking punishment. But more of that elsewhere. I am at present concerned to show that the real cure of "unruliness" is not authority, but a sense of responsibility in the person concerned, so that he may frame his own "system of rules for conduct."

But in addition to the too amenable and the frankly unamenable, there is a third, very difficult type of person, a typical product of the too authoritative regime. I refer to the person who has learnt that important imperative of authoritarian discipline "Thou shalt not be found out." Such a lad was Arthur Ford. Like all lads of this type he was charming and polite, always clean and tidy—a perfect gentleman to all intents and purposes. His chief trouble was that he was always getting the sack from his jobs for being "bone idle." Not, I venture to say, because anyone ever saw him doing nothing. We never did. But because he never did anything *except* when he was under observation. He was never to be found among the rebels at Hawkspur Camp, but when there was any window-smashing going on it was a pretty safe bet that Arthur was doing a little quiet encouraging, while loudly decrying such wicked hooliganism. It has a very salutary effect upon such persons to learn that they are their own authority, and no one can find them out except themselves. Or that if there is an authority outside themselves it is not some official who has to be beguiled and tricked, but the other fellows with whom they are living who, if they go beyond a certain point, will express disapproval. In

Arthur Ford's case my colleagues and I just refused to watch him. Ron Urwin, who at that time was in charge of construction work, asked him if he would like to build a goat shed. He had never done such a thing before, but, polite as ever, he said he would if Ron Urwin would "give him a few tips." Ron drew a plan and said, "There you are—get on with it. You're doing this on your own. Anything you want to know about it I'll tell you, but you must ask me first." The goat shed was at the far end of the field well away from observation. Arthur settled down to have the time of his life. We practically never went near him, though on the rare occasions that anyone did go near him Arthur was always hard at work. Not for one moment did I allow him to imagine that I did not think he was hard at work all the time, and I even went so far as to say that the camp needed a few more people who could be left to go ahead with the job. But he learnt his lesson, and when he discovered that there was really no one to see that he got on with the job except himself—he got on with it, and did a fairly workmanlike job. The only complaints he heard about the slow progress of the job were from his fellow members.

Each of these three types of person has got to learn that he cannot just leave the responsibility for his behaviour to someone else, and in our system of sharing the responsibility for the government of the camp we have always that end in view.

Our Camp Council combines the two main functions of government—judicial and legislative—always with the proviso that its functions and procedure may be changed, on its own decision, at any time. That is to say, it makes laws (except when it makes agreements) and it enquires into any breaches of laws that may take place. About some things it accepts the common usage of polite society without actually making laws. For example, I believe there is no law about property, but there is what might be described as a common law tradition against stealing. I do not mean there is tradition against *committing* a theft, quite the contrary. But stealing is something that can be "brought up" at the Camp Council. In addition it is a permanent committee of ways and means charged with the duty of arranging day-to-day events, programmes for entertainments and so on. Its income is derived from taxation—at present 5d. per head per week, or a farthing per working hour—paid by everyone in the camp, and a first charge on its funds is the maintenance of any who have not earned enough to pay for their own board and lodging. It is also responsible for the replacement of any camp property wantonly or carelessly broken, lost, or stolen; the upkeep of windows, crockery and cutlery; and the provision of "social amenities." They may, of course, recover from the persons responsible any sums they have to pay out in respect of loss or damage to camp property.

In practice the Camp Council is not so much a governing body as a vehicle for the expression of public opinion. It has always taken the line that if it says a thing should be done, then that ought to be enough, and it has, from the beginning, been not merely reluctant to inflict punishments, but definitely opposed to it. And though I do not expect to be believed, I can say with my hand upon my heart that I do not think this is due to my influence—but rather the contrary. But the Council has found that public opinion to be effective sometimes has to be represented by a token. The history of Camp Council penalties is rather interesting. At one time we had a committee of four which met daily to transact the day-to-day affairs of the camp, the Council meeting as a legislative assembly once a month. I took the chair at this committee, and for reasons of my own I deliberately "worked on it" until they became pretty well my "yes-men." They were having a good deal of trouble with a young man who refused to do any work, and repeatedly asked him to come to the committee to tell them *why* he refused to work, but he wouldn't do that. So, taking their courage in both hands they fined him 6d. for contempt of court. Then George woke up. "You can't do that," he said. "Well, we have done so," said the Committee. So George got to work. There were conferences and discussions in the bunk-houses. There was a special Camp Council, and what fun we had. I had, anyway. It was a serious matter for George—25 per cent of his pocket-money. He had the camp solidly behind him. The Committee were told they were a lot of weak-kneed, yellow-livered yes-men, Wills's pets, did whatever I told them, but this time Wills wasn't getting away with it, and their decision was revoked by an enormous majority.

Next Camp Council the Committee was abolished. So ended, ignominiously, the first effort at punishment. I must confess that I was in a measure responsible for this effort to introduce punishment. I wanted to make quite sure that the failure of the governing body to use punishments hitherto had not been due to a slavish following of my principles, nor to simple lethargy.

Another attempt at introducing punishments was in connection with kitchen duties. We do not employ a paid cook, so we have to arrange the kitchen work between us. The cooking is not much objected to, but few people like getting up before everyone else, especially in the winter, and very few enjoy washing up. We have tried many different systems, but the one usually in operation is a rota of two each day. The difficulty was to enforce the rota. Often breakfast was late. Sometimes one of the two people appointed just refused to do the job. I remember one day on which there were no meals at all in the real sense—the food was issued by the Quartermaster, and those who wanted it cooked, cooked their own. Hardly a Camp Council took place without heated discussion on this point, until at last, in desperation it was decided that a fine of 1 shilling should be inflicted on anyone dodging his kitchen duty, even in part. They thought their troubles were ended, and things went smoothly for a few weeks. But then a popular member and one capable of throwing his weight about dodged his turn—and the law was rescinded. Oddly enough, that was about the end of our trouble on this question, and for two years now there has been no trouble at all over kitchen duties—it is just accepted by everyone that who ever you are and whatever other offences you commit, you owe it to the community to take your turn in kitchen—no one ever dodges it.

The final effort to introduce punishments came up after the camp had been running nearly two years, and the rule then made has never been rescinded. Ostensibly it is a rule to prevent bullying, but actually it is a rule which gave Camp Council, at last, real authority. The weakness of the Camp Council hitherto had been that the bullies, not always overtly, but none the less certainly, had tended to get their own way. There has always been less fighting and bullying than one would expect, but at a pinch it was always the toughs who got their own way at Camp Council. Whenever—or almost whenever—anyone threw his weight about it was discussed at Camp Council (I saw to that, if the aggrieved party was afraid to) and a pretty strong public opinion was expressed against it. But it still went on, and the bully could defy the Camp Council with a certain amount of impunity because no one dare suggest drastic measures against him except the staff, and they had reasons of their own for not doing so. I have my own way of dealing with bullies, aimed at removing the fear which makes them bullies. But it takes a long time to effect a cure by that means and prevention must, if possible, be used in the meantime. There developed quite an epidemic of bullying, and at last in desperation a law was made that anyone using physical violence, with whatever provocation, should automatically be fined a shilling. Naturally it was tested. The small fry realized that if they dared to face the consequences and insist that the law be carried out, it might mean the end of bullying. They were quite right. They stuck to their guns, inflicted the fine the first time it was earned, and there was an end to bullying. I do not mean that no one ever in the heat of the moment strikes anyone. But there is never deliberate violence. I do not believe that is because of reluctance to pay a shilling. It has now been reduced to 6d., and is just as effective. I believe it is because those who tend to bully feel that if the community is prepared to go to the length of inflicting a fine, then it really does feel strongly about it, and it is thus the public opinion rather than the penalty which holds the bully in check. This is what I meant when I said some pages back that the Council found that the mere expression of public opinion was not enough—it had to have a tangible expression.

This suppression of bullying gave new life to the Camp Council, and a new dignity. No one now is afraid to say just what he thinks, and the Council has real authority. It still inflicts no punishments except for bullying, and in this it follows the established practice of National Governments, i.e. its severest penalties (in our case its *only* penalty) are directed against those who would undermine its authority.

My attitude to all this as Camp Chief is a very detached one. I have a dual role which sometimes causes misunderstanding. As a member of the community I am anxious to prevent the social evil of bullying, by any reasonable means available. As Camp Chief I am anxious to relieve the fear and unhappiness which makes a boy a bully, and the two attitudes are mutually exclusive. But by a happy legalistic device I am able to oppose the community in its indictment of any individual without compromising my duty to the community. If penalties are being used care must be taken that they are not unjustly awarded. The accused must be defended. And by the decision of the Camp Council I am Counsel for the Defence in all cases except when I am one of the principals. It is very astonishing to a new member who has offended against some law (for I have unofficially extended my advocacy to non-punishable offences when it suits me) to find that the people accusing him are his fellow-members, and the one person who is trying more than anyone else to excuse his action is the boss! This is just one of the ways in which we get the boy who comes to the camp to see that we (that is my colleagues and myself) are really on his side, and ready to approve of him.

CHAPTER FIVE

Camp Council—continued

> "I mock thee not, though I by thee am mocked,
> Thou call'st me madman, but I call thee blockhead"
>
> WILLIAM BLAKE

REALLY to appreciate our Camp Council you ought to attend it—preferably as a fly on the wall, as we are apt to be self-conscious when there are visitors. As that is not feasible, I propose to give, as far as possible, a verbatim account of a meeting.

Most of us are sitting round our dining-tables, which are just a couple of trestle-tables (which we made ourselves) with green lino. on the top. They are arranged like a T, and the officers sit across the top of the T. Mac is in the chair. He is one of our senior members and is an excellent chairman. My wife is Secretary just now, and the Treasurer is a young man who left his job in a city office in order to come to the camp for a year or two because he felt he needed it. The Vice-Chairman is a young man of 19. Shall we call him A.B., to save the trouble of inventing names?

"All right," says Mac, "will you chaps round the fire come to the table, please?" (There is a rule that all must sit at the tables during meetings.) There is a little grumbling and protesting, but they all come eventually and Ruth gives us each a typed agenda.

Camp Council

MAC: I declare the Camp Council open. One—Apologies. Any apologies?

RUTH: Yes. Len sends an apology, but doesn't give any reason.

MAC: Two.—Minutes of last meeting, please.

RUTH: Minutes of meeting held umpteenth of which month, 19exty.

1. An apology for absence was received from Bryn.

2. The Minutes of the last meeting were read and approved, with one alteration.

3. The accounts were read and approved after 2d. had been re-imbursed to Camp Council for Len's bed. (Beds must be made in one's own time, before the day's work starts. If a bed is not made in time the cleaning orderly makes it, and Camp Council is charged with "Man's time making so-and-so's bed." It is up to Camp Council to get it back from the offender if it thinks fit. In this case Len had been the offender, but he pointed out that he was on kitchen duty that day and therefore entitled to make his bed later on. So Bods had to pay 2d. back to the Camp Council.)

4. E.F. suggested that in future all fines be paid to the Treasurer at a meeting of the Council. This was agreed. The Treasurer reported that one fine had been paid, and one instalment. (This was intended to relieve the Treasurer of the unpleasant duty of going round begging people to pay up.)

5. Owing to the present debit balance it was agreed that any member losing time should refund 10 per cent of money lost to Camp Council, until it was solvent. (This is incomprehensible to the outsider. If a member was absent from work for, say, an afternoon, he got no pay for that afternoon.

That means he has not enough to pay for his board and lodging, so Camp Council has to pay what he is short. Camp Council could not recover it all from the offender, because his total pocket-money for a full week only amounted to half a crown, so they recovered a proportion of it.)

6. Len made a charge of assault against G.H. (a German refugee) on behalf of I.J., as I.J. had not done so himself. G.H. admitted shaking I.J. because the latter had said his word was not to be trusted, but claimed that it was none of it very serious. The Camp Council finally agreed that this should not be regarded as an assault, and the matter was dropped.

7. It was agreed that wheels should be put on the present barrow. A.B. to do so.

8. I.J. reported that a back number of his *War Illustrated* had disappeared from his bunk. He brought all he had to prove one was missing. The matter was discussed, but it was not felt that anything could be done in the matter.

9. W. D. Wills asked if anything had been done to pay I.J. for damage to his bicycle by other people. I.J. reported that he had been paid two-thirds of the damage and would soon have enough to pay the bill.

10. It was agreed that a bolt be put on the bath-room door.

11. W. D. Wills pointed out that the French Class had been continued for six months in spite of the gloomy forecasts some time ago at Camp Council. He suggested that E.F. be publicly congratulated on keeping the class going so long. The Camp Council agreed to this.

12. R. Wills asked for the loan of a bowl from the bath-house for the week-end. This was agreed.

MAC: These minutes in order?

RUTH: There's another lot yet—about G.H.'s tie. Shall I read them now?

MAC: er—well—no—one at a time I think. Are these minutes in order?

C.D.: I move they be signed.

SEVERAL VOICES: Seconded.

K.L.: All right, stop yer shovin'.

MAC: Order, please.

K.L.: Well, stop him from shovin' me off the form.

MAC: All in favour? Well—now we'll have the other lot, please.

RUTH: Minutes of special meeting held such and such a date. This was called to enquire into the disappearance of a red tie belonging to G.H.

SEVERAL VOICES: Hoorray.

RUTH: He claimed that it had been taken from his bunk.

ANON.: Ha! ha!

A.B.: He's found the damn thing now.

E.F.: Mr. Chairman, the tie has now been found.

MAC: Will you please save your comments for the right place?

A.B.: Well, he *has* found the damn thing, hasn't he?

MAC: Under matters arising from the minutes, please.

RUTH: It was decided to search the bunks and Mac and M.N. were appointed to do so. The tie was not found, however, and the Camp Council decided they could do no more in the matter.

MAC: These minutes correct?

CHORUS: Sign 'em, and let's get on.

MAC: Right. Three. Matters arising from the minutes.

I.J.: Well, Mr. Chairman, I have to report that on Thursday last I was looking through my *War Illustrateds* and I found that the missing copy had been replaced. (Loud laughter.)

A.B.: Put down that G.H. has found his ruddy tie. Don't think it was ever lost myself. Oh—and put down that I've put the wheel on the barrow. Might as well get a bit of credit.

BUNNY: I should like to report, Mr. Chairman, that the bolt has been put on the bathroom door as suggested at the last meeting.

WILLS: I should like to enquire, Mr. Chairman, what is the cause of all this efficiency.

A.B.: Pipe down, Duke.

MAC: Nothing more arising from the minutes?

RUTH (*softly*): Thank you for the bowl. It's back now.

MAC: Four. Treasurer's report

M.N.: We started with an adverse balance of 6s. 5d.: Lamp Steward 3d., Wireless Steward 3d., wasted food 4d., maintenance charges 3s. 11d., as follows:—A.B. 11d., E.F. 6d., Dick 2s. 6d. (This means that these three, having "lost time," had had to call on Camp Council to this extent to make up their board and lodging money. You have read in last week's minutes that the Council is now recovering 10 per cent of this. You will see it in the credit side, below.) Income—Taxation, 6s. 11½d., Fines, Dick, owing five weeks, 3d. Then we recovered 10 per cent of what we had to pay out in maintenance for A.B., E.F., and Dick—4½d. Total on the credit side, 7s. 7d. So the debit balance has been reduced from 6s. 5d. to 3s. 7d.

ANON. (SEVERAL): Hear, hear.

MAC: Any remarks or questions?

Q.R.: Yes. What's this about wasted food?

BODS: (Quartermaster): I'm sorry to have to speak about this again, Mr. Chairman. The Constitution says the Camp Council is chargeable for any deliberate damage to camp property. I've spoken several times before about people cutting the crust off both ends of the loaf at supper-time. Now somebody is cutting the sides off as well so that practically the whole of the inside gets wasted. That seems to me to be damage to camp property, and in charging only 4d. I'm letting you off lightly. If you want to find out who is the responsible person and make him pay you back, that's up to you. I think everyone knows who it is.

DICK: I'm not the only one.

BODS: I haven't mentioned any names. But since the cap seems to fit you I don't mind saying that in my opinion you know more about it than anyone.

A.B.: Make him pay up.

DICK: What about you? You're as bad as me.

A.B.: Liar.

MAC: Order, please.

E.F.: Mr. Chairman, in view of the fact that more than one person may have contributed to this unfortunate contretemps, I think that on this occasion we should let the matter pass.

WILLS: And let the Camp Council pay for the food that some careless blighter's chucked away?

E.F.: On this occasion, yes. We might take further action if it occurs again.

MAC: Do you move that?

E.F.: Yes, Mr. Chairman.

VOICES: Seconded.

MAC: That seems to be agreed. Anything else about the Treasurer's report?

Q.R.: Yes, Mr. Chairman. Why should the Lamp Steward get 3d. for looking after the lamps when someone else has to light them nearly every night?

A.B.: Oh! look who's trying to get 3d. a week now!

Q.R.: Well, if I had the job I *would* do it.

A.B.: Oh yeah?

MAC: I think there's something in what Q.R. says, but perhaps if we were to ask A.B. to attend a little more carefully to his job . . .?

A.B.: All right, Mac, I'll be a good boy in future. Anything to stop that twerp from getting the job.

MAC: Well, we must get on. Stone picking. Mr. Wills?

WILLS: Well, it's like this, Mr. Chairman. Camp Council's hard up. The camp needs a road. We have plenty of stones on the field, but picking them up's a lousy job and if we offered it as ordinary work there wouldn't be any takers—not at the normal rate of pay, anyway. I wondered whether it would be any good if I offered to pay ½d. into the funds of Camp Council for every bucket of stones collected off the field. Outside ordinary working hours, of course. If a party is organized, for example, on Saturday afternoon, I should be very glad to join it. And it did occur to me that some people—without mentioning any names or looking at anybody—owe rather a lot to Camp Council in fines. Perhaps we could allow them to be paid off in this way? But that's another matter.

A.B.: What a lousy idea! Just like you, Duke. Why can't we keep the money ourselves?

WILLS: I'm only trying to help Camp Council's funds. You can take it or leave it. But it has the advantage of giving you an opportunity of feeling self-righteous on two grounds at the same time. You're helping to make the road without any hope of personal reward, except the remote hope of keeping your shoes clean; and at the same time you are by your labours reducing the deficit in the Camp Council accounts. Two birds with, if I may so put it, one bucketful of stones. As the chief moaner about having no accumulator for the wireless and no daily paper, I should have expected you to leap at it, A.

A.B.: Not me. Too much like work.

(There was a lot of talk about this, the newer members being anxious to find out where the catch was, and what *I* should make out of it. But they accepted it in the end.)

MAC: Number 6. Bryn?

BRYN: What time are we supposed to be called in the morning, Mr. Chairman? Sometimes the kitchen people call us about quarter-past seven, some call us about five to eight, and when Bunny's on kitchen he never calls us at all. When *are* we supposed to be called?

BUNNY: Mr. Chairman, I protest!

A.B.: Fat lot of good calling you. You never get up, anyway.

BRYN: That's what *you* think. And it's no good calling you because you might just as well stay in bed for all the good you are when you've got up.

A.B.: Bet I do a damn sight more in a day . . . .

MAC: All right now. Save that for later.

E.F. (who is something of a Mrs. Malaprop): Well, Mr. Chairman, I think that in the interest of improved punctuality and general camp convenience a specific time should be hereby promulgated for the benefit of all concerned, and I therefore . . . .

A.B.: *For crying out loud*, cheese it. I move that the kitchen people call us all at 7.30.

CHORUS: Seven-thirty, seven-thirty.

MAC: That seems to be agreed. Now number seven—a charge of assault. G.H. *versus* S.T. All right, G.H. (Both parties are German refugees.)

G.H.: S.T. have provocated me. He have used bad words with Elizabeth and no German boy can allow this, so therefore am I provocated.

MAC: What do you say, S.T.?

S.T.: I have not done this. He is a liar. He have hit me.

WILLS: Mr. Chairman, I'm afraid I'm responsible for this charge being brought, so perhaps I may give my version, as the English of both parties is limited.

MAC: O.K.

WILLS: I found them locked in a death-grip in the kitchen, and when I prised them apart G. said he was going to murder S.T. I asked him why, and he said S. had been extremely provocative, his honour was at stake, and he had no alternative but to wallop S.T. It seems that S.T. had been asking Elizabeth the meaning of certain indelicate words, G. claiming that S. knew they were improper. So I told him that if S.T. had done something that was not in order he should raise the matter at the Camp Council, and have it dealt with there. The charge is therefore not strictly one of assault so much as of provocation.

G.H.: I have not understand. He have provocated me.

WILLS: Yes, that's what I said. He used bad words to Elizabeth and you said no German boy could allow that.

G.H.: He have call me a dirty Jew also. He have used bad words with Elizabeth.

Q.R.: Well, Mr. Chairman, I don't know whether S.T. was asking Elizabeth the meaning of swear words or not, but if he was, he got the idea from G.H., because I have often heard him doing the same thing.

G.H.: This is a dirty lie. No German boy will do zis sing.

WILLS (sarcasm being his besetting sin): Except S.T., of course.

S.T.: Mr. Chairman, he have hit me mush—many—times. I will fined him.

MAC: At present we're talking about you provoking G.H. If you like you can bring a charge of assault against G.H. afterwards.

S.T.: I will do zis. I will fined him . . . .

Much more in this vein. The upshot of it all was—quoting from the minutes—"after much discussion Camp Council dismissed the charge on the grounds that (*a*) G.H. had done much the same sort of thing himself when he first came, and (*b*) it wasn't conclusively proved that S.T. had not been encouraged by G.H. The Camp Council also decided that a counter charge against G.H. should be made by S.T. on the ground that G.H. had hit him. It was agreed that G.H. be fined 6d. for hitting S.T., when he knew that Camp Council expected differences to be settled there, and not by violence."

MAC: Eight. Apologies. E.F.?

DICK (suddenly waking up): I've paid my fine.

A VOICE: So what?

MAC: We're not dealing with that now.

DICK: Well, you said we had to pay all fines at Camp Council, but I've paid mine to the Treasurer.

MAC: We finished with all that a long time ago.

DICK: What do I care? I've paid my fine and it ought to go in the minutes.

MAC: Pipe down, Dick. This is E.F.'s item.

DICK: I'll no' pipe down. I want it in the minutes.

RUTH (saving the situation): All right, Dick, I've put it in the minutes—"it was reported that Dick had paid his fine, but not at the Council meeting."

MAC: Now then, E.F. What's this about apologies?

E.F.: Well, Mr. Chairman, there are some gentlemen who profess to be members of this assembly who continually absent themselves from our conventions without presenting adequate or suitable excuse or reasonable cause . . .

BRYN: Too bad, E.F. I've come to-day, you see.

E.F.: Who said I was talking about you?

BRYN: Ha! . . . Ha!! . . . Ha!!!

E.F.: If I may be permitted to continue, Mr. Chairman, I propose that in future all apologies for absence from this meeting be accompanied by a valid reason, otherwise the offending party to be fined for his absence. . . .

VOICES: Oh, shut up . . . Cheese it . . . Boloney, E.F. . . You can't get at Bryn that way, etc.

(This proposition was the result of a personal feud.)

MAC: Any seconder?

VOICES: NO.

I.J. (E.F.'s boon companion): I second it.

MAC: All right. It's seconded. All in favour . . . one, two . . . Against? Sorry, E.F. Not carried. That's all then. Camp Council is closed.

CHAPTER SIX

Punishment

. . . . it wouldn't do
For people such as me and you
Who very nearly all day long
Are doing something rather wrong

H. BELLOC

ONE day "Yus" went berserk. I forget what had annoyed him, but he threw a saucepanful of potatoes at someone, and when others attempted to restrain him he shook them off, picked up a heavy form six feet long and threw it at someone who had sought the safety of the other side of the dining-table. He was just looking round for something else to throw when I gave him a hearty clip on the jaw, which I followed up with a shove in the midriff which put him in a corner of the room with me in front of him, and there I stayed until his ardour had cooled.

This was not punishment, and "Yus," when he came round, was the first to realize it. It was just the quickest way to end an intolerable situation. A smack on the jaw in the heat of battle was neither here nor there to "Yus," and he was probably glad I stopped him from making a worse fool of himself. It did no harm, saved a lot of damage, and I would do the same thing again in like circumstances.

The only other occasion on which I struck a camp member

I have never ceased to regret. In this I succeeded, as punishment very often does succeed, in achieving an immediate end; but only at the cost of postponing indefinitely the ultimate end of the camp training. It was T. Miner again. Ever since the camp started its members had been gentlemanly and courteous to my wife. I do not mean that they were prigs or parlour gentlemen. They did not rush to open the door when she was going out, nor always relieve her if they saw her carrying something. But she was seldom left for long without a seat, and above all they invariably matched their conversation to their company. One day I began to realize that they were becoming rather lax about this last, and I was afraid (I use this word advisedly—it is fear that makes the martinet) that this excellent spontaneous tradition was breaking up. Then I heard T. Miner using language that was really deplorable in my wife's presence. She didn't care two hoots, but I was so proud of this tradition that I didn't want to see it spoiled—quite forgetting that its whole virtue lay in the fact that I had had no hand in its creation. So I asked T. Miner to step outside, and suggested to him that he owed Ruth an apology. He was very truculent, and was damned if he'd apologize. I pressed him, and he said, "What'll happen if I don't?" I replied that I might forget myself, so he challenged me to forget myself forthwith. It is with shame that I record this childish conversation, and I do so only because of the valuable lesson involved. Having spoken like a child, I acted like a child, and punched T. Miner on the jaw. He was quite ludicrously astonished, and the degree of his surprise is the measure of my criminal stupidity. This was a youth whose need, above everything else, was to feel secure. Over a period of many months we had been working hard to provide this feeling of security (see pp. 66 and 67) and here, in five seconds, a year's work was destroyed—or at any rate, seriously damaged. Miner, the "tough guy" of the camp, spent the afternoon on his bed, weeping—and never again used an unsuitable word in my wife's presence.

What was worse, no one else did either. But whereas their previous gentlemanliness had been natural and spontaneous, it was now unnatural and forced. Whenever anyone's conversation began to be "dangerous," Miner would say, "Look out—Wills will sock you one."

Miner had been positively seeking punishment all the time he had been at the camp. Seeking it in the sense that he wanted to make quite certain that at last he was loved and secure. If we still refrained from punishing him in spite of this and that, then we must indeed love him. "Difficult" behaviour is very often just this testing of security, and if in the test we are found wanting, we are failing in our job.

But punishment is sought for other reasons beside the testing of security. There is also the seeking of punishment in order to "square the account."

I have spoken of my old schoolmaster, of hated memory, who used to say, "I don't mind you chaps at the back there having a little chat while I'm teaching. Not at all. Go ahead and enjoy yourselves. But remember that all the good things of life have their price, and the price of talking while I'm teaching is two strokes. Come out here and pay up." This is a most pernicious doctrine, though it is one which, with its practice of penance, orthodox Christianity has done much to foster. It is pernicious because it implies that two wrongs can make a right—that an evil done to one person can be rectified by an evil done to another. Hence I may make myself a nuisance to my neighbours as much as I like if I am prepared to pay the penalty. The reckless young fool with more money than sense pays his 40s. or £5 for dangerous driving with a perfectly easy conscience. He has bought a little exhilaration and excitement just like he might buy a pair of bootlaces, and is often quite indignant when he is also admonished by the bench. In the same way the difficult child or youth finds in punishment a means of wiping out his last offence, so that the account is squared, and he can start on the next transaction. I do not mean that a boy will come and say, "I have done so and so. Punish me"—though I have known that happen more than once. It is not as direct and conscious as that. The idea of penance for failing to reach a certain standard of conduct is so deeply ingrained in us that we are vaguely unhappy until the penance has been paid; but the idea of seeking pain is so contrary to our nature that the pursuit of punishment is often carried on unconsciously. Sometimes it is no more than a slip of the tongue that "gives the game away," but frequently I have had boys go out of their way to bring their derelictions to my notice, in the hope that I shall wipe the slate clean by punishing them in some way. Indeed this type of behaviour was so commonplace that one ceased to remark it, and it is difficult to recall instances. One boy went into my wife's bedroom at the White House and stole a brooch, which he openly wore about the camp. She sent him a little note telling him he could have it as a keepsake. Another boy, temporarily living in London, stole a wallet containing £5. I asked him to come to the camp to see me about it. There was nothing to stop him refusing to come, but he came—a cold, uncomfortable journey of 3½ hours—and denied vehemently ever having touched the wallet. I argued, pleaded and begged, but he was resolute in his denial. (I am not as a rule concerned very much to make a person "own up." But a great deal hung on getting this affair cleared up.) He even denied it while he had the wallet in his hands, toying with it in front of me! Many a schoolmaster who has to interrogate boys suspected of misdemeanours preens himself on his skill in "tripping up" the suspect. He would have less occasion for pride if he realized how earnestly one-half of the victim is co-operating with him! Even when the punishment is death, the criminal will often do something to ensure that he is discovered, or to ensure that it is possible for him to be discovered by an astute person. Theodore Reike gives some interesting examples of this in his fascinating book *The Unknown Murderer*.

Then there is a third kind of punishment-seeker—the kind who seek punishment for its own sake. I do not refer now to the masochist, though many of the type of person to whom I now refer may well have masochistic tendencies. But masochism, like sadism, is a much abused word, and by refraining from its use I shall avoid its misuse. The people I have in mind are the people with a strong "guilt feeling," who commit punishable offences in order that they may, by punishment, assuage this feeling of guilt. They have "committed adultery in their hearts"—adultery or some equivalent sin, often of an homosexual nature, and they cannot be punished enough. The most outstanding example of this was a young man who always spoke of his mother with the utmost contempt. His attitude to his mother was, I'm sure, largely responsible for his guilt feelings, which were intense. You may believe, if you wish, that this guilt arose from the fact that he had not for his mother the affection and respect which polite society insists are a mother's due. Or you may believe, as I presume you will if you are a Freudian, that his overt attitude to his mother was an attempt to compensate a too great affection—a mother fixation, which was itself the cause of the guilt feeling. But the feeling was certainly there. accompanied by the most erxtraordinary efforts to get punishment. He very quickly broke every rule and regulation the camp had, and I did all in my power to prevent the community punishing him. Certainly I never punished him myself, though I was pretty nearly exasperated sometimes. He wantonly destroyed, for no reason at all, a book which he knew to have a very great value for me. He maligned my name and those of other campers about the countryside. He even tried to bring contempt upon the camp by dressing himself in ridiculous clothes, and visiting middle-class neighbours thus dressed. They would, of course, assume—and he would help them to assume—that his condition was due to our neglect. So determined was he to be punished that he actually tried to make me believe that he had committed other people's crimes. One day a rucksack, belonging to one of the boys disappeared. I was determined to find out who had stolen it, not in order to punish the culprit, but because this seemed the only way of getting it back. Every time the matter was discussed in public this young man said something to direct suspicion to himself, until at last I was convinced that he was the culprit, and told him so. I charged him with the theft, and we had many long arguments. His contributions to these discussions were such remarks as, "Even if I *had* taken it I wouldn't tell you where it was," and "If I own up, what will you do to me?" alternated with violent denials. It was a long time before we discovered that he knew nothing whatever about it!

It is manifestly futile to punish people who are seeking punishment, whether they seek it in the course of testing their security, or to "square the account," or to assuage their guilt feelings. You may say, "But these are abnormal people —they must be few and far between." My reply is that they are indeed abnormal (though not so very few and far between). But so are all delinquents in this particular—that they fail to react as normal people are supposed to react to punishment. I have already said that you might almost define a criminal as a person for whom punishment is ineffective. How many fathers have said to the magistrate, "I've thrashed him again and again, and it seems to have no effect"? Here I am assuming what some would deny, that punishment is harmless and useful with some people. But I only assume that. I do not assert it, as I am concerned at the moment only with that class of person known as delinquent, and I am convinced that with them it is useless.

Even if your offender is not positively seeking punishment, there are still plenty of reasons why he should not have it. I will not give statistical reasons. They have been available in Home Office publications for years, and have convinced no one, not even the Home Office, so why should they convince you? Examine such scraps of case-histories as you will find in this book, and ask yourself if punishment is morally justifiable, even if you can convince yourself that it might be useful. Can you punish a boy whose thefts are a symbol of his desire to be loved? Do you think it useful to punish someone who has been so ill-treated and bullied that he goes through life with an almost irresistible desire to do as he has been done by? One of the most futile of theories about punishment is the theory that if a child is cruel it must be made to realize what pain *is*. Too often it is because they realize very well what pain is that they are so interested in inflicting it. Who are the people who are so anxious to have flogging retained as a statutory penalty? Excluding the women of the Conservative Party, who must come in a separate category, they are in the main the old Blimps who puff out their cheeks and say, "Why damme, sir, when I was at Harron I was thrashed, and a good thing too. Look at me to-day." Consider Slosher Hare. His father was a drunken bully who used to thrash the whole family every Saturday night. His mother was, from all accounts, no better than she should have been, and when he was about ten he was sent to a "Home" (O blessed euphemism!) in which order was maintained by a foster-mother with a cane which she frequently used. When he was nearly fifteen he was sent to a large Farm Training Colony, where he got in with a gang who committed petty thefts in the neighbourhood. All except Slosher were sent to Borstal; he was sent "home," and his guardians sent him to Hawkspur Camp. He was about sixteen when he came to us, and I want you to remember that the two most important things in his background were (*a*) He had never been loved in any real sense. (*b*) He had been thrashed, bullied, and kicked about from pillar to post; but more than anything else, thrashed. He was a merry little imp, and almost the first thing he began to do after he came to us was to repeat his father's conduct. I don't mean that he got drunk; but he did bully anyone who would take it, often people much bigger and older (though softer) than himself. He was constantly pilfering—generally elegant articles of clothing of a kind which he, in his Institution life, had never possessed. He was frequently in trouble with the Camp Council but they were not very successful in getting him to mend his ways. He could be very littled touched by punishment or by public opinion. He needed affection, and we set out to give it to him. He said to me one day, "I was down past the White House last night." "Ah yes," I replied, "did you call in and see Ruth?" as if that would have been the natural thing to do, which it wasn't, because, while we often had campers there, we tried to discourage them from coming except by explicit invitation. He said he hadn't, so I told him he should—any time. So he "dropped in" at all times and seasons. Sometimes, if I was sleeping out, I would come down from the camp at about 11 o'clock hoping for a peaceful hour before going to bed, and would find Slosher there, having a heart to heart chat with Ruth, who would be wondering how she could get him out without appearing to do so. Very often there would be no one in when he called—we would both be at the camp—and then he would take a few cigarettes in lieu (we never locked the doors). After some months one of his chief victims said, "Do you think that if you're kind to Slosher he'll stop hitting people?" I admitted that I had some such idea, and prepared myself for a scornful retort. But it didn't come. Instead I was told, "It seems to be working, doesn't it?" How I treasured up those words! But let me say in parenthesis a few words to those who have "tried kindness but it didn't work." I've met them often. They come to me after a lecture and say, "Mr. Wills, what would you do in a case like this?"—(as if anyone can *ever* say what he would do "in a case" until he has lived with the "case" a few weeks; and even then what would be right for me might not be right for someone else)—and they unfold a tale of some unhappy person's misdemeanours, ending with, "I've tried kindness, but it doesn't work." Kindness isn't a patent medicine of which one takes a couple of doses just to confirm one's suspicion that it is useless. It must be "instant in season and out of season." It "suffereth long." It must be continued for months and if need be for years. You cannot eradicate the effect of ten or fifteen—or more—years of brutality by a couple of weeks of "kindness." It must be applied in something of the spirit of that faith which can remove mountains.

When Slosher had been with us just over a year he said he wanted to leave. I was not too keen on the idea because although I could see a great improvement I was not sure that it was sufficiently consolidated. But he was. He was sure he would be "all right now." His mother found him a job, he went, and he has been getting on famously ever since.

A person who has to endure punishments provides himself with protection. He surrounds himself with a "tough crust" in order that our violence, whether physical or not, shall hurt him as little as possible—just like we used to rub resin on our palms when I was at school.

But our work is not concerned with the tough crust—it is with the soft core. We can never reach that core while we are provoking the subject to a hardening of his "crust." Once we touched Slosher's "soft core" (and he was attending the Poetry Group before he left) it was not long before the trick was done. But we should never have touched it if I had punished him.

One final word about Camp Council punishments. The reader will be wondering—perhaps impatiently—why, if I am so opposed to the use of punishment I can allow, indeed foster, an organization which has the power to inflict punishments. There are several answers, but perhaps the simplest, as well as the most important, is this. I am concerned with ultimate ends, which punishment does nothing to further—the removal of "bad" traits and the building up of character. The Camp Council is concerned only with immediate ends, which I do not deny may often be secured by the use of punishment. We go about our separate jobs in our own ways, and everyone realizes that we are doing separate jobs. Not that the Camp Council has much use for punishment. I have already shown how little it is used. But so far as it is used, it is used in the main for non-moral offences, such as breaches of the Camp Council's regulations. As a rule, when the Camp Council begins to realize that it has a case before it in which the person concerned is so to speak displaying his symptoms, they are quite happy to leave him to me. Thus they might deal with a person for not working, but leave him to me for stealing; or they might deal with another for stealing and leave him to me for not working. I do not mean that there can ever be a hard-and-fast division like that, and often we both "treat" the same offence. But very often, after a time they begin to recognize tactitly what a person's principal weaknesses are, and to realize that I have the matter in hand, though they may not understand exactly what I am doing.

And, of course, there is all the difference in the world between a penalty imposed arbitrarily by a person in authority, and one imposed by one's peers in a democratic assembly. That is so well known and so widely recognized that I need not dwell upon it here.

CHAPTER SEVEN

Work and Wages

"Mr. Emmanuel Crayfish maintains
'Start a house with laying the drains' "
HUMBERT WOLFE

ONE day a young man came up to me and said, "No more work for me. I've finished. I'm not going to do another stroke as long as I stay at the camp."

"O.K.," I said. "I'll keep you to that."

For several days he was, if such a term is permissible, aggressively idle, and no one said a word. If I happened to see him as I was going out in the car to do some shopping I very often took him with me, just for a ride. No word of blame or reproach was uttered, at any rate by the Staff. We said, "If you think you're better off doing nothing than doing something—well, good luck to you."

Then one day I caught him furtively picking up an axe to chop up some wood for the fire. "Here," I said, "are you a man of your word, or aren't you? You told me you weren't going to do another stroke of work as long as you're at the camp. What about it?"

He uttered an unprintable word, threw down the axe and walked off. I kept this up for about a week until I saw that he had had quite enough of idleness—then I let it drop. He never again threatened to do no more work.

Work and Wages

At that time there was no payment for work done—each lad received 2s. a week pocket-money irrespective of what he did. Later, we amended this for reasons I shall explain, but even then a newcomer was told that he need not do a stroke during his first month if he didn't want to. Issy Abraham was delighted when I told him this. His trouble had been simply that he wouldn't work. When he had been at the camp about ten days we had a visit from Dr. Franklin, who asked Issy, as a new boy, how he was finding things. "It's lovely," he said.

"In what way is it lovely?"

"Well, you needn't do any work at all if you don't want to. I never did a stroke at all last week, but I'm doing a bit now. You get fed up doing nothing."

Now, six months later, Issy is one of our most reliable workers.

It is the fashion nowadays to poke fun at the Victorian interpretation of the Christian ethic, particularly in respect of sexual morals; but no one seems to bother much about attacking the pernicious Christian fable about the origin of work—how it is a punishment inflicted on man as a result of the misconduct of our common ancestors in the garden of Eden.

We are all brought up to believe—even before we experience it—that work is something which all sensible people try—if at all possible—to avoid. We are so conditioned as to have an unpleasant emotional response to the word work. Before we know how to react to a thing we must find out whether or not it comes into the category "work."

Going round with the corporation dust-cart emptying dust-bins it has been decreed comes under the heading "work," and is therefore regarded with horror. Hurling oneself into several inches of slimy mud on a cold winter afternoon, while about twenty other hefty people pile themselves on top of you, the same mysterious authority calls "play," and millions of men (of whom I am proud to confess I have never been one) persuade themselves without any difficulty that they enjoy it. This seems to me to be a lot of nonsense. I am not saying that lots of work isn't unpleasant, and if I had to choose between going on a six months' cruise in the Mediterranean and hoeing mangels for six months I am sure I shouldn't choose the hoeing. But I do say that the vast majority of people are much more unhappy in their work then they need to be, just because of this anti-work conditioning, and the prejudice against work which is instilled in us quite irrespective of what the work is.

At Hawkspur Camp we try to break down this deplorable prejudice. That is one of the objects of our occupational programme. I suppose the other principal objective (though, of course, they are closely connected) is to show what work means to the community—why we have to work at all from the standpoint of society as apart from our need as individuals. To take the second aim first—that is perhaps the most important reason that it is Q Camps and not Q Homes. We twentieth-century people are in the fortunate position of being able to take for granted the toil of thousands of people who work for our convenience. By merely pulling the plug (and this is one of the greatest boons of civilization) our homes and highways are kept sweet and clean from human refuse. In camp we have to carry it away every day in buckets and bury it in a hole in the ground, and we are all in the camp long enough for the novelty to wear off and feel quite grateful for w.c.s when we get the chance to use them. I give this rather crude example because as I say, the water-closet is one of the very great blessings of civilization that we have to do without in camp. But the same sort of thing applies in lots of other ways. We don't get our milk from a nice clean bottle, placed by a benevolent providence on the doorstep every morning (though we do have to fall back on that occasionally). We get it from the goat. And if someone doesn't milk the goat we don't get any milk. You see the sort of thing. It's just jolly fun for a fortnight in the summer and you're sorry to get back to civilization. But when you've enjoyed it all the summer and all the winter you begin to realize the comforts and delights of this sniffed-at civilization are something worth having, and that they have come into being through that kind of genius which is connected with taking pains and working hard. And you learn to a certain extent how it works.

It might perhaps help to show how we achieve this end of demonstrating the back-stage of civilized life and the other end of breaking down the prejudice against any thing called work if we just take a look round the camp on a typical day, and see what fifteen to twenty people are doing.

Two of them are "on kitchen." They got up at 6.30, lit the kitchen fire, prepared breakfast and washed up afterwards. They will prepare dinner and serve it and wash up afterwards, likewise for tea. To-morrow two other people will do it. This is something everybody takes a turn at, and we have never had a professional cook at the camp.

One will be "on day-room." He sweeps out and tidies up day-room and bunk-houses and the camp site generally. He digs a hole and buries the contents of the latrine buckets. He scrubs the kitchen floor. Here again someone else will be on the job to-morrow and the only people who don't have a turn on day-room are the ladies.

Three or four will be on the gardening squad growing vegetables strictly for our own consumption, making flower gardens and lawns for our own delectation and that of our visitors. Three or four again will be in the construction squad. "Construction" is an all-inclusive term. It means primarily erecting buildings for our own use. All our buildings were erected by camp labour except one small sectional building which was needed in a hurry the first winter. Our day-room, also, was not built to our own design—it was an old Army hut given to us by King Alfred's School and which arrived in rather a dilapidated condition. But the two bunk-houses, each accommodating ten men, the goat shed and the chicken houses, the bathroom and the office and stores, were all entirely built and designed at the camp. The last two we are particularly proud of. They were both designed by "Bunny" Barron and, of course, erected under his supervision. The bathroom is quite an elegant little building in bright colours. It has a bath-tub and trickle bath with h. and c. all put in by camp labour. Water comes from a spring in the middle of the field. That, if I may digress further, was an interesting story. While we were still in the tent stage, we wondered what we should do about water. For the first week or two we used a spring on the side of the road which involved carrying each bucketful about 250 yards. We were told there was "plenty of water" on our land if it could be found, so we set about finding it. Right in the middle of the field was a patch where the grass was a much richer green than anywhere else. Here, with much excitement, we dug. Four feet down water began to well up, and amid cheers an underground spring was discovered. This has been the camp's water supply ever since. We dug a hole into which we sank two concrete rings each measuring two feet deep and three feet in diameter. These were given by a friend who was farming in the neighbourhood. This was always referred to as "the well," though in reality, of course, it was a small reservoir. When we erected the bathroom there was again much excitement over water. Our crude and amateur surveying seemed to indicate that the top of our new building, some hundred and fifty yards away, would be lower than the well, which meant that water transport could be left to gravity. In due course a pipe line was laid from the "well" to the side of the bathhouse. It only remained to connect the bathhouse end with the internal system, and turn on the stop-cock at the well end. "Never mind about connecting up for the moment," we said, "turn on the water. If we're lower here, the water will run out." We all stood round the open pipe while someone reluctantly detached himself to run over and turn on the water. "Here she comes," he shouted, and having turned on the water rushed back. No water! "suck the pipe." No good. Nothing came. We must be higher than the well, after all. Too bad. We shall have to incorporate a semi-rotary pump in the system and pump it up every day. So we put in a semi-rotary pump, connected everything up, and began to pump. While someone pumped we all stood round and listened to the hollow sound of water falling—for the first time—in the cistern. After a time the pumper stopped for a rest. But the water didn't stop running and it hasn't stopped yet, except when the tanks are full.

I allow myself this digression to show not only how

purposive but also how exciting as well as how educative it all is.

To return from my digression—that is the construction squad building our camp, and repairing it as need arises. They also make any articles of furniture that are needed. Their first job was to make a carpenter's bench, and from that bench the whole camp has grown.

Then you may find one or two engaged on weaving. We haven't made our own clothes yet (though every man has to repair his own), but we made all the curtains for our last new building and several have made themselves ties and scarves. It is useful to find for oneself what lies behind so simple and every-day thing as a piece of cloth; and there is opportunity for the education of taste in choosing a design. Another man may be working in the office. We have usually had at least one man who wanted to do office work. My wife teaches them shorthand and I dictate non-confidential letters to them. Another may be engaged on casual labouring and working on our embryo road, or digging a refuse dump. We may see the stockman grooming the goats or feeding the hens. And by then we have seen pretty well everything.

When we first started we said in effect, "this place exists purely for the benefit of the members. Between us we must do the work that needs to be done, but as everything that needs to be done is for your own benefit, *you* can see that it *is* done. The Q Camps Committee provide experts, to advise and supervise, but *you* must provide the labour."

It didn't work very well. With a normal community it might have done, but ours wasn't normal. Sometimes we had lads who were in such a neurotic state that they *couldn't* work. The other fellows complained and I had to defend the idleness of the neurotics. On the whole, they were remarkably tolerant of non-workers, but presently they began to say, "He isn't doing anything, why should I?" And there was a good deal of slacking. Even when a chap had learnt that work can be pleasant and enjoyable, it is *still* very annoying to hear someone strumming on the piano during working hours.

So we lifted the whole responsibility for seeing that work was done out of the hands of the Camp Council—but with their full consent and approval. They were told that they must apply for employment to one of the "gang bosses"—to Bunny in charge of construction, or to Elizabeth in charge of the garden, or to Len in charge of the laundry, or Bods in charge of casual labour and odds and ends. Each man was paid a shilling an hour for a twenty-hour week (i.e. mornings only), of which 9d. was retained for his board and lodging, a penny was credited to his clothing account, so that when he wanted new clothes he came not as a suppliant having to prove how long it was since he had a pair of shoes but as a person expressing a right; three farthings went in taxation to the funds of the Camp Council and the remainder went into his pocket. Thus, if he lost an hour the 9d. that should have gone towards his board and lodging had to come, so to speak, from the P.A.C. (the Camp Council) and he lost his hour's contribution to taxation, clothing and pocket-money. Apart from the incentive to work for its own sake there were these two other incentives at work, an individual and a social one. His pocket suffered and he became a charge on the public funds, thus incurring the displeasure of his fellows, because the more the Camp Council had to pay out in "Poor Law," the less it had to disburse on more desirable things such as a wireless set and ping-pong table (see Chapter "The Camp Council").

We found this an admirable arrangement. It is all very well to talk about the joy of labour, but you can never find there is such a thing unless you first start labouring, and many people need an arbitrary incentive to make that start. It had the further advantage of showing, in terms of hard cash, the effect on society of people refusing to contribute their quota of work—how people who do not support themselves have to be supported from the public funds to the detriment of other desirable social services. And finally, this scheme had the great virtue that it placed funds—and thus tangible responsibility—in the hands of the Camp Council, which benefited greatly by it.

All that, as I have said, applies to the mornings only. In the afternoons the work programme is much the same, but there is no pay—in the afternoon the only incentives are the love of the job and a desire to contribute something to the general well-being. Some work just as hard in the afternoon as in the morning. Others who have still much to learn, do not.

So the days and weeks pass by, each man contributing a quota to the general good, learning new skills, acquiring confidence in his new-found knowledge and increasing capacity, becoming self-reliant by learning to do everything for himself and, above all, by seeing the fruits of his labour, discovering that he is a person, and that when he pulls his weight it really makes a difference.

CHAPTER EIGHT

Fathers and Sons

"If the man who turnips cries,
cries not when his father dies,
'Tis a proof that he would rather
have a turnip than his father"
SAMUEL JOHNSON

IT became almost a commonplace at Hawkspur that if the Camp Chief went away there would be trouble. On one occasion half the camp went careering round the countryside in the camp car. On several occasions work was virtually suspended for the week. Once windows were smashed, another time the local public-house was broken into—and so on. It worried me a good deal until I realized the cause, though even now it tends to make my holidays a trifle uneasy and I am never able to be away from the camp for more than ten days at a time.

It is not due to any magical influence which is removed when I am removed, nor is it in the least a reflection on my colleagues. It is not because Wills is away, but because Camp Chief is away. It would be exactly the same whoever was Camp Chief, unless he were someone quite unsuited for the job. It is because the Camp Chief is the father figure, and to many of the young men who come to Hawkspur the father is a very important figure. I suppose everyone knows nowadays that a very high proportion of young delinquents come from homes in which the parent-child situation is not as it should be—one or both parents dead, parents separated, foster-parent, parents quarrelling, and so forth. From time to time I have run through our members to see in how many this situation was to be found, and it occurs with such regularity that I have come to the conclusion that where the parents seem quite normal it is only because we do not know enough about them!

The parent child relationship is a complex and delicately poised affair, which can go wrong at a large number of different points. One of these is the father-son relationship.

Freud tells us—if I may paraphrase him in idiomatic English—that sons have very mixed feelings about their fathers (he calls it ambivalence). The boy tends to begin by disliking father for trying to monopolize his mother and for restricting his liberty, but of course he is taught at a very early age that he must love his daddy and not have these naughty feelings towards him. So the dislike is forgotten almost as soon as it is conceived. For that is all repression really is; an active forgetting. As a rule that is the end of it—it is forgotten and never heard of again. The son is helped to forget his dislike of his father because as he approaches "middle boyhood"—ten, eleven, twelve—he begins to become conscious of his destiny as a male. He looks round for an example of what he is to become, and of course finds it in the nearest male to hand, his father. So now father has become loved hero instead of hated rival. As he grows up and meets other people he gradually gets his beloved hero into proper perspective until as he himself reaches maturity his father is just another man.

That is the normal state of affairs, so normal as to be very unusual, and so simplified as to be almost untrue. But that is the general idea. Sometimes the boy doesn't follow the track I have indicated, and then, if there is a serious divergence, there may be trouble. Off-hand I can think of a round dozen Hawkspurians who seemed not to have been able to effect the correct relationship with their father—and we at the camp had to suffer the consequences. There are two main divergencies from the normal. One is the failure to cope successfully with the early father hatred; the other is an inability to find in the father the hero figure which most boys need.

The first group are the ones who give the Camp Chief a rough time. They are just running over with hatred of their fathers, which is coupled with intense feelings of guilt because they have been taught how wicked it is to harbour such feelings against father. In many cases the conflict thus set up brings about what is commonly known as a "nervous breakdown." Often it occupies so large a proportion of the mental space and energy of the unfortunate person concerned that all other aspects of his life and work suffer, and he becomes a "problem." Sometimes they transfer their hatred of their father to someone or something else of whom that father reminds them, someone in authority. Thus they may, in a religious environment, become God haters, in a capitalist society Communists, and I presume, in a Communist society anarchists. I am not suggesting that every atheist and every Communist is so because he is a father hater, but that element is present perhaps more often than is sometimes imagined.

When these father haters come to the camp they have a fairly simple solution to their difficulties. They "displace" their father hatred on the Camp Chief or the Camp Council, in which they can then indulge themselves without the guilt feeling attaching to real father hatred, as it is not nearly so wrong to dislike the Camp Chief, and they can usually find ample reason. They can thus get rid of all their pent-up emotion and gradually acquire a more normal attitude to their environment. It is interesting to develop the history of one or two of them.

Sydney Harman came from a family in which the parents had been daggers drawn almost ever since they were married. In such families it is not surprising if the sons never come to have a normal relationship to their father. They begin—as we all do—with the mother as the centre of their affection, and with the best will in the world, it is very difficult for the mother to be other than pleased if the son seems to find the same aversion to the father as she herself has acquired. That at any rate is what happened to Sydney Harman. I will not trace all his history, which was a complicated and difficult one with other significant aspects besides the one I am now writing, but at any rate he suffered two of the consequences to which I have already referred—he was "under the doctor" for a "nervous breakdown" and he was an ardent Communist. That he was interested in Communism merely as a revolt against authority and not as a political system was very soon made clear. When he arrived at the camp and found how democratic it was, and how little use we have for personal authoritarian discipline, he was delighted. This fitted in admirably with all his beliefs and ideals and he set out to show his "social sense" and become a leader of the community. He saw what was wrong with the place (i.e. other people's social sense was defective) and he set to work with a will to put it right. He said there was no reason why things shouldn't "go" and he was going to do his best to make them go.

But of course the life of a loyal, co-operative, law-abiding citizen was not what Sydney *needed.* He needed to continue to displace his "father hatred"—to revolt against authority—and we very soon found that Sydney far from being on the side of the angels was absolutely against the government wherever any traces of government could be found. At first his animosity against me had a rational basis. Whenever the Camp Council put forward any good idea, Wills, he said, prevented it being put into effect. This was of course quite untrue. But it is an accusation I am always having to face, because we always have at least one Harman in the camp. When he was there it was particularly strong because we had three or four of them together. I asked repeatedly for examples of this obstructionism, but none was ever forthcoming. Presently we had a change in the constitution and an executive committee was set up to meet daily, the Camp Council to meet only once a month. Here was something for Sydney to attack, and he attacked it with venom. So fertile was he of ideas as to how the committee ought to do its job that he was soon elected to it. This so restricted his field of revolt that it was more than he could bear. He resigned, refusing to give any reason. The occasion of his resignation is interesting and illustrative. I had a letter from an ex-member saying "the next time you come to town in the car, could you bring Eddy to see me?" So the next time I went to town I took Eddy along with me so that he could spend a few hours with his friend. Even before we started off at eight o'clock in the morning news was brought to me that Sydney was resigning from the committee. The following day I enquired further into it. It was quite clear from what I believe are known as unofficial sources why he had resigned. Wills had had a day off, and had given Eddy a day off, and they'd both gone to London for the day in the car, which was gross favouritism, and he wasn't going to stand for it. That was the story he put about, but he absolutely refused to give it as his reason for resigning. He would not give it as his reason because he feared that if he did I should reply that I went to London on business and that I had taken Eddy at someone else's request. He would then have had no reason for resigning, and he did so want to be an outsider and a rebel. And so he became so to speak an outlaw. He was recognized as being anti-Wills and by now he no longer troubled to find rational excuses for his animosity. Wherever there was any trouble or smashing up, or hooliganism, or anything that could be calculated to be a nuisance to Wills—no matter who else it annoyed in the process—Sydney Harman was there. At last he was leading a relatively satisfactory life—hating his father (in me) without the necessity for feeling guilty about it. Whenever he was particularly obnoxious to me, I was obnoxious in return, because if I had remained sweet-tempered and kind he would have started feeling guilty. By this means I was able to feed him enough excuses for his animosity, while retaining in between bouts a perfectly friendly attitude. I will not continue further the story of Sydney Harman because it has other aspects to which I may refer elsewhere. What I have said of him is typical of several of the lads who came to the camp, and it is something which must never be forgotten by anyone proposing to take a "fatherly" attitude to young offenders. It is not necessarily only the boys who manifestly like and admire the worker who are getting what they need from him, though generally one would hope to secure the boy's affection eventually. Indeed if the worker has become a surrogate father he should expect the attitude of antagonism gradually to give place, if things are following their normal course, to one of admiration and affection.

This development was clearly to be seen in the case of Tom Beeley, to whom I have referred elsewhere. His father was quite clearly (if my information is correct) a simple martinet. Every moment of Thomas's time must be spent in approved activity with approved associates, under pain not only of paternal displeasure but also of punishment. The family all used to go on holiday together. Months before everyone knew that on August 6th they would all go to Rhyl for two weeks, staying at such and such a place, exactly what the programme would be for each day—Monday morning Dad and Tom will go fishing, Monday afternoon the family will go bathing, Monday evening all go to the pictures, and so on. Every moment foreordained and prevized by a paternal benevolence. And Mr. Beeley was surprised when his son grew up devoid of backbone. He would have been even more surprised if he could have seen the seething cauldron of hatred and frustration in Tom's mind. The unconscious hatred was so strong that it had to be strongly compensated, and Tom was apparently a most devoted son.

When he came to Hawkspur Camp it was like opening the sluice gates. Here was someone in precisely the same relation to him as his father, but by whom no filial love was expected. The hatred and venom directed against me was something quite dreadful though I hasten to add that it was entirely surreptitious—he was usually perfectly charming to me, and it was not until he started abusing me to my face that I felt that progress was being made. The bunk-house at night was the place where he gave vent to his feelings about me, and so intense and spiteful were they that they brought tears to the eyes of another boy whose feelings for me had reached the second stage, e.g. of affection. His hatred was all inclusive and embraced the whole camp. He was having psychotherapy from a doctor in London to whom he used to give the most dreadful accounts of the privations he had to suffer at the camp. The doctor asked him whether he had discussed these things with Mr. Wills, and he had to confess that he hadn't. He was persuaded to do so, and I told him that if he didn't like things he should get them changed. And he did. He needed a lot of quiet pushing from behind, but he was ultimately responsible for quite a number of changes at the camp. I think that this opportunity to give positive and constructive expression to his feeling of revolt was very useful, particularly in lessening his sense of failure and frustration. Helped, of course, very materially by psychotherapy as well as by the episode of the girl friend of which I give an account later on, his attitude to me underwent a subtle change which was just beginning to make itself manifest when he left. Right up to the time he left he still insisted (as all father haters do, as it justifies their attitude to me) that I had a grudge against him, but his subsequent history is revealing. When he went home he lived at first with his family, handing all his wages over to his father each week and receiving so much pocket-money back (aged twenty-three). Within eighteen months we find him living—for the first time in his life—in open and successful but quite reasonable and unimpassioned defiance of his father, while writing fairly frequently to me. He went into lodgings, he married a girl his father disapproved of, and his attitude to me until the time of his marriage was warm and friendly. I do not think he particularly hates his father now. He has broken away from him and got him into proper perspective, and being happily married no longer needs either of us.

There were others, on the other hand (and I rejoice to say that so far they have always been in the majority), who are not troubled by any need of a father surrogate to hate, but who have been unable to adjust themselves to the second stage I referred to in the father relationship. They have been unable either because they had no father, or because he was an inadequate father, to create for themselves a "father hero." These seem to me (I have never seen this tendency referred to by anyone else) to be going through life with a picture of the ideal father, whom they have been denied, in their minds, and as soon as someone comes along who is prepared to be friendly and has anything like a paternal relation to them, they are prepared to find in him all the virtues they have ascribed to their ideal father.

It is of course just another aspect of that tendency of which Lord Baden-Powell made such brilliant use when he devised the Patrol system The young male adolescent loves to be one of a gang following devotedly a revered and respected leader. I very well remember the veneration in which I held my patrol leader when I was a Boy Scout, and later as a patrol leader myself, how I hung upon the lips and copied every trick and foible of my Scoutmaster. That is the normal sort of development and the less adequate the father is, the greater is the need of a leader figure outside the family. If the father is grossly inadequate then the need for a surrogate father may become pathological. The successful worker with boys must be quick to notice the symptoms of such a relationship and must readily react in a sympathetic way. Often a careless rebuff will upset such a boy for days on end. I remember one occasion when we were rehearsing a play, and one youth failed dismally to learn his words. At last I became annoyed and said if he hadn't got the guts to put his nose to the grindstone for an hour or two and learn his words, what the hell? or words to that effect. I could have kicked myself as soon as I had uttered the words and the boy was upset for days despite my efforts to repair the damage.

The youth who has adopted one as a father is usually recognized by his tendency to adopt one's style of dress and speech, though this is not, I find at least, always easily recognizable, and very often it has had to be pointed out to me by my wife. Of course, when a lad whose name is John Smith signs himself inadvertently John Wills, the meaning is fairly clear, but it is not often as easy as that. What makes it more difficult is that very often the boy is so shy about, and ashamed of, his affection, so afraid of appearing "daddy's boy" to the others that he will take pains to conceal it, and even indulge in abuse of his loved hero at every opportunity. Such cases must be very carefully distinguished from the real "hater." The hater's prime need—for the time—is to work off his hatred and if he gets a little abuse in return it doesn't matter very much, it will serve to lessen his guilt. The *apparent* hater, however, who is merely concealing his too great affection, needs primarily affection, and that he must have. A sharp word spoken in haste will cause him days of distress. Only experience teaches the worker to distinguish the abusive boy who needs to hate from the apparently similar boy who needs to love, though he will do well to look for the symptoms I have just referred to—the tendency to ape the worker. We had one such boy at the camp. Very few people suspected that he had any other feeling for me than loathing but his clothes were most amusing. If I wear shorts I effect rather short ones. His were so short as to be almost indecent. Sometimes if I were going out I would change into a pair of flannel trousers. Shortly afterwards he would be seen in flannel trousers. During the spell in which I was trying to make myself somewhat more presentable, I took to wearing a tie instead of an open-necked shirt. So did he. His pullover must be the same colour as mine even if he had to steal one to achieve the desired result.

As I have said, the boy in this stage has transferred his affection (or a proportion of it) from his first love object (the mother) to the second love object—the father or father-surrogate. This transferring of affection from the primary love object to another is known in psychological language by exactly that term. It is known as the transference. It is of the most profound importance socially, educationally, and therapeutically. Without it very little success can be hoped for in the sort of work about which I am writing. It must have a chapter to itself.

CHAPTER NINE

The Transference

"It may be that no man would be a hero to his valet.
But any man would be a valet to his hero . . ."

I SHOULD like you to cast your mind back if you can to what I was saying about Charley Horsfall in Chapter Three. I talked a good deal of what may have seemed to you esoteric nonsense about Authority speaking now through my lips, but previously through someone else's.

Now Charley, like most of us, loves and is loved. He started his love life by loving his mother, and presently he was to "transfer" some of that affection to his father. His mother, and later his father, were the boundaries of his horizon. All good things came from his mother—food drink, and physical comfort. She and his father were omnipotent and all-wise. Since they were the only fount of knowledge all that came from them must be true and beyond question. At a very early age they had implanted in his mind ideas of right and wrong, good and bad, and had associated with those ideas further ideas about penance and punishment. These ideas had been implanted by the Supreme Authority, whose word at that time could not be questioned, and they were therefore planted firmly and ineradicably, nourished and fertilized by the strength of his affection for them. It may be that as Charley grew older he began to find that mother and father were after all not all-powerful and all-wise, and he may well have come to question their authority on all manner of things. But the ideas which had been implanted during the non-questioning stage had already reached the full growth of axiomatic truth. Charles does not say, "This is right because mother and father say so." He says, "This is right because I feel it to be so." He has no recollection of the source of his convictions. He recollects only the feeling with which those convictions are charged. He does not realize that the reason he feels a thing so intensely to be right (or wrong) is that he associates it unconsciously with his attitude to his parents, and his feelings for them, which are a mixture of love, respect, and awe. Primarily love, for the mother, and love transmuted into respect and awe, for the father. They still exist, in the background of his mental life, in their original stature as lawgivers and authorities on everything. When they were the boundaries of his emotional life they created in his mind an attitude to certain things, and that attitude is for all time imbued with and supported by the authority they had at the time the attitude was first created.

I have a horror of swearing. Conscious ratiocination since I grew up has convinced me that bad language, while perhaps vulgar, is nothing more. Even blasphemy is mere words, and is surely regarded by God with the tolerance one gives to the fractious and frightened child who says he doesn't care for anybody. But the amount of horror I feel when I hear anyone really letting himself go is comparable only to the horror I feel when I hear, for example, of some particularly barbarous atrocity. No amount of reason can prevent this feeling surging up, even though I know that its source is this early father which is still alive in my mind and emotions.

So with Charley's attitude to punishment. At a very early age he has been taught that we should be punished when we are naughty. And then he has been made to feel very very naughty *without being* punished; or has committed crimes which he was taught to regard as very dreadful (swearing, perhaps!) and then punished only lightly. So—to express it crudely—all his life he has been trying to "catch up" on his punishment. I know this to be true in Charley's case because he has told me how, when he was a child, his father used to lecture him interminably about his misdemeanours, creating a tremendous feeling of guilt and unworthiness—but very rarely inflicting any punishment. There is a lesson here for those who dislike punishing children. Do not make Mr. Horsfall's mistake of substituting tremendous feelings of guilt. If you must lecture, lecture about the futility or silliness or inconvenience of the misdemeanours—not about their wickedness.

This spell, then, if we are to help Charley, must be broken, though to break it really effectively would call for something very much like witchcraft. We should have to send Charley back to his childhood, peel off all the accumulated layers of knowledge and experience, and have his parents, in all their pristine authority, undo the damage they had done. Putting it another way, we should have to take Charley back beyond the stage where his parents (particularly his father) became the awe-ful lawgiver to the stage where the relationship was primarily of love. This is not possible, though something akin to it can be, and is, sometimes done. I suppose we may say that in a cosmic sense Jesus did it. He said, "You regard God as the dreadful and jealous giver of laws who sets you about with laws and prohibitions and will punish you for your offences. He is not that primarily; He is really a God of Love." That, however, by the way. So far as individuals are concerned, it is done in psychoanalysis. To be successful the psychoanalyst has to get the patient to transfer to him something of his early feelings for his mother, and he can then speak to the patient with something of his mother's authority —an authority created solely by the child's affection for her, and not adulterated by the later awe and dread for the father. I am not suggesting that that is the whole of psychoanalysis. But I believe it is true to say that that is a very important part of it.

But of course others besides the psychoanalyst can secure a "transference" and thereby secure something of the early authority of the parents. When the subject transfers to psychotherapist, teacher or leader the affection he had for his mother we call it a positive transference. When he transfers that transmuted love, consisting now of dread and awe, or even hatred, which he later felt for his father, we call it a negative transference.

If we secure a positive transference we may not have the *same* authority as the parents, because the child has now acquired the capacity to reason, and will receive any instruction with a certain measure of healthy scepticism. But our words will carry such authority as to be subjected to far less criticism than that of a person to whom there is no transference. Even the negative transference may be made use of, as I have indicated in my chapter on "Fathers and Sons." But it is the positive transference that is of the greatest value in the kind of work we are now discussing.

Charley Horsfall—to return to him at last—had made an incomplete transference to me, and I was therefore able, at any rate, to offer battle to the Old Man still persisting in him—he was able to accept a certain measure of my attitude to things.

The transference may be brought about by the most silly and trifling of things. It may be that I hold the loaf the same way as some lad's mother when I cut it, and that simple fact may cause an unconscious association and, if other circumstances are ripe for it, a transference. This, I imagine, must be the explanation of "love at first sight." However, we cannot, at Hawkspur Camp, study each member's mother and copy each characteristic in the hope of effecting a transference. But there is one characteristic which most mothers have—and which certainly all children seek in a mother—and that is a loving attitude. Many people of the kind that comes to Hawkspur Camp have been disappointed in their mothers. They are prepared to lavish all the affection their mothers spurned on anyone who is willing to love them. In general, then, the attitude most likely to secure a transference is an attitude of affection. But young children also feel respect and admiration for their parents. Anyone then who earns the respect and admiration of another is in a favourable position for securing a transference.

It is, as I have said, rarely difficult with the type of person we get at Hawkspur Camp to secure a transference (though sometimes it may be a negative one) because so often their relationship with their own parents has been interrupted before the time when they would normally pass beyond the stage in which the parents are the chief love object. A.B.'s mother had died. He had done a little pilfering and was extremely indolent. He began to effect a transference to Bods, but Bods was rather afraid that, at that time, this might cause difficulties with another youth who was making claims upon him, and deriving great benefit from having those claims satisfied. So, in (apparently) pure fun he started referring to A.B. as the Duke's pet. When I came in at tea-time Bods would say "Come on, A.B.—here's the Duke. You're his pet—hadn't you better pour some tea out for him?"—and so forth, to the great amusement of everybody. But so great was A.B.'s need for a transference that this wholly jocular assumption of its existence was enough to create it. Although A.B. laughed somewhat shamefacedly at all this fun I was fortunately able to see that it meant something real to him—and from that time on we are able to see an improvement. From that time everything I said and did and believed had for A.B. an enhanced authority, because he had transferred to me something of the attitude he had once had to his mother.

It is quite impossible to over-emphasize the value of the transference, and it is equally impossible to give a complete picture of it at work, because its influence colours the whole of what one does. In a community, too, where many need to effect a transference and there are only two or three upon whom the transference can usefully be made, there will be much jealousy and unpleasantness. These feelings are much more pronounced in an environment where the transference is being deliberately exploited for the therapeutic ends than they are in a normal environment, and they raise many serious problems. When a boy made a transference to me in my bad old disciplinarian days I was flattered, I accepted his admiration condescendingly and was very careful to see to it that there were no relaxations of discipline in *his* favour, in case I should be able to accuse myself of the dreadful crime of favouritism. For the transference often arouses a "counter transference" and—even if one is not a disciplinarian—one has to be careful to avoid becoming emotionally bogged. I well remember how once Teddy B. created a scene in the kitchen, where he had been sent to do special duties for a spell instead of working in my squad, to which he really belonged. The scene ended by Teddy throwing, I think, a scrubbing brush at "Ma," the cook's wife. When threatened with expulsion from the kitchen (to work in which was considered a great privilege) he went to the length of *swearing* at Ma—"I *want* to bloody well get out—I want to get into Mr. Wills's squad again" (for I was a Mister in those days). So far as I remember, his only reward for this touching piece of loyalty was a telling-off, though the whole matter was no concern of mine. How different would my attitude to Teddy be now! I should have arranged for him to stay in my squad as soon as I was aware of the transference or, if that were impossible, have done what I could to mitigate the agonies of separation from me. One of the things which prevented me from acting thus sensibly was of course the thing which prevents thousands of other people in the same position from taking an intelligent line. It was a false modesty which was really a colossal conceit. It would have seemed in me a lack of modesty to do anything which implied that I realized this lad was fond of me. It is, after all, not considered quite the thing to say "Yes, of course, so-and-so is very fond of me." But the only reason we think it not modest is that we are conceited enough to imagine that we are loved because of some remarkable virtue we possess, which no one else has. It is undeniably true that some people have to a remarkable degree the faculty of inspiring affection in others; but in the case of an odd casual transference like this, it was just as likely to be due to some repulsive little habit I had which reminded the lad of someone in his own (probably unsavoury) family. I expect I used to lick my thumb when dealing cards. Or more probably it was the way I ate my sausages. Before he came to Z home, of which I was in charge, Teddy had been in X home where, with certain companions, he had been found to be incorrigible. He was therefore transferred to Z. On his first morning with us I called him to the Staff table at breakfast-time and made, in public, some heavily facetious remarks. It was Sunday morning, and during my three and a half years at that institution we had two sausages for breakfast every Sunday. Teddy knew nothing about me until then except my reputation as a bully, and had been dreading coming into my home. He wept after I had chaffed him—and was a changed character from that day. Probably his mother used to bisect her sausages laterally before eating them!

So Teddy just worshipped me from afar, and gratefully accepted such small crumbs of recognition as he was able to extract from me, without causing any bother to anyone except himself. Fortunately, although he had been "naughty," Teddy was not really a specially "difficult" youth, and the transference could, so to speak, do its work without any help from me—in spite, indeed, of my pig-headed and wilful hindrance.

How different at Hawkspur! Most of the inmates there have a transference to the Camp Chief of a greater or lesser intensity, and even a person with a negative transference can be intensely jealous. I am thus in the centre of what one intelligent person described as an "emotional vortex." Everything I say or do is carefully watched by several pairs of ears and eyes, and if I address two words to one person I must be careful to suggest a game of ping-pong to another, offer a cigarette to a third, and give another a smack on the back. But even so, it is impossible to distribute one's favours equally, and there is always jealousy and backbiting. Very often one must "favour" one person at the expense of others, and damn the consequences. There are various people concerning whom at various times I "balanced all, brought all to mind," and decided that the good consequences likely to accrue to that individual from "favouritism" were so great as to outbalance the evils caused to others by it. Raymond was in this category. During my absences from the camp (which were much more frequent than I care for) he found life almost unsupportable. He would do no work, "shriek about all over the place," as Bods described it, and generally behave in a very hysterical way, making life for everyone in the camp very difficult. So, if I were going out for a few hours in the car I would take him with me; and if I were leaving the camp for my weekly "day off" I would say "if you find things getting too difficult come down to the White House—you know we shall be glad to see you (which was no less than the truth, in this particular case at least). The jealousies and difficulties caused by this treatment were so great that I did sometimes wonder whether it was worth while. My colleagues were dubious, and one at least was frankly sceptical. There was even a special Camp Council about it, called, if you please, by the one boy who, at that time, was noted for the violence of his negative transference! Very portentously Sydney Harman said he wanted to raise a question of great importance and common concern. What was wrong with this camp was that Wills had favourites and it was his opinion that if I treated everyone alike things would be very much happier. Very mischievously, I fear, I said I was surprised to find that *he* pined for my favours. I had always gathered that if there was one person in the camp whom he wished to have less to do with than anyone else, that person was the Camp Chief. This, of course, stuck a pin in a very tender spot and made Sydney extremely angry. When he had calmed down he tried to make it clear that it was not of himself he was thinking—such base, selfish motives were far beneath him—he was thinking of others, of the good of the camp as a whole, and of justice in the abstract. He demanded, in the name of justice, equal treatment for all. "That," I replied, "within the limits of my human frailty, is exactly what I try to provide." Scornful laughter from Sydney and several others. "Not uniformity," I said, "but equality. If several of you were ill and the doctor came, you would be justified in demanding that you were all given a bottle of medicine, or whatever it was that your condition called for. But you would look pretty silly if you started kicking up a fuss because Raymond, who has one complaint, is given some physic which tastes sweet and you, with another, were given something that tastes like prussic acid. And you look pretty silly now, only you don't know it. I don't give everybody the same physic. I try, so far as I can, to give them the kind of physic they need. Needs vary a good deal, but my attitude to them all is the same—so far as I can, I try to supply them. You, Sydney, go up to London every Tuesday to see Dr. G. Do you insist, in the interests of abstract justice, that we all come with you? Jim Payne gets painting lessons. Do you demand painting lessons for everyone? Why is it that it is only this particular need that I am not allowed to supply?

For we have had this trouble before. It is not very long since everyone pretended to be upset because T. Miner was, they said, Wills's pet. I have even been accused by some of making a pet of Sydney Harman. In the future there will be others with needs of varying kinds, some of whom will need the kind of treatment Raymond is getting now—and so far as possible, all their needs will be supplied . . ." But, of course, reason is of little avail against emotion, though I like to feel that all my arguments were not entirely wasted.

Those times spent with Raymond used to be devoted partly to the discussion of his immediate difficulties, but chiefly to talking about books and poetry and pictures. I can see him now, lying on my hearthrug while I read "We who with songs beguile your pilgrimage, and swear that beauty lives, though lilies die . . ." None of these things had meant anything to him before. Now they meant pretty well everything to him. Any doubts I may have felt about spending so much time and attention on Raymond have long since been dispelled by the sequel. Alas, I cannot give you that sequel because if I were to do so any of Raymond's present circle of acquaintance, chancing on this book, must immediately recognize him. Let it be sufficient that Raymond, who came to us from a mental hospital, has now found his niche and is getting along very well in it. And that is all because I was not afraid to exploit a transference at the risk of "favouritism." If Q Camps had achieved nothing else, Raymond's history alone would have justified its existence.

But of course Raymond is only one of many, of whom I will quote only one, in this case a transference to my friend and colleague Bods. Bryn was illegitimate and his mother, when she married, did not marry Bryn's father. Her husband, however, a middle-class professional man, was like a father to Bryn, and one would have imagined, from her attitude, that it was the mother who bore the step-relationship. Towards the end of his schooldays Bryn began dimly to realize that his mother (though he would never have been as articulate as this about it) hated him as evidence of her early sin and his step-father only loved him for his mother's sake. He started pilfering and later became a "girl-hunter," in his late teens living up to everything his mother hated in herself and feared for in him. He came to the camp and "fell for" Bods. He completely relived his emotional childhood starting at scratch and achieving something very much like maturity in a couple of years. He was at first completely dependent emotionally on Bods and even for a time shared Bod's tent instead of sleeping in the bunk-house. What a fuss the others made about that! Bods consulted me about it. I told him I was a trifle dubious about it, but if he thought it was right, then it was right, even though by now the jealous ones were openly making unpleasant suggestions. But he grew out of this dependency, adopted all Bods's ideas about everything, particularly about sex (which had been his principal trouble) and the desirability of stability in one's sexual relationships. He is now happily married and is I think a stable and dependable man and husband.

It is easy in retrospect to write about various people having effected a transference, but it is by no means an easy experience to undergo. The psychoanalyst in his consulting-room secures a positive transference from his patient. That is to say the patient's libido, his vital force, his emotional power, is directed to the analyst. It is the analyst's job to manipulate these highly emotional currents, and the consulting-room must have at times an extremely tense atmosphere, in which one false move by the analyst might cause the deepest distress, and perhaps much harm to the patient. But the analyst just sees one patient for an hour at a time. Imagine if you can the tense atmosphere when a person is *living* with a number of people who have this attitude (though to a somewhat less degree, it is true) to him—and who are quite conscious of each other's attitude. The atmosphere becomes at times so tense as to be almost unbearable. Not that the Camp Chief of Hawkspur Camp is consciously probing in the murky depths of anyone's unconscious. That would I think be a mistake, even if I were qualified to do it. I was told by someone who had been prominently associated with the Little Commonwealth that Homer Lane's downfall was largely attributable to the fact that he "analysed" the children. I think that may well be true. The emotional vortex of which he is the centre is already violent enough without any attempt to stimulate the objects whirling around in it. If psychotherapy is necessary in any case it should I am sure be carried out by someone quite outside the "vortex"—if possible in an environment quite outside that of the camp or institution.

I conceive the job of Camp Chief of Hawkspur Camp to be somewhat analogous to that of a hospital matron. The matron and her staff have a working knowledge of the ills of the flesh, they know what kind of atmosphere is most conducive to recovery from those ills, and they know how to co-operate intelligently with the physician. So with us, except that where the hospital staff are concerned primarily with physical needs, we are concerned with things of the mind and spirit. I imagine that in many cases, once the physician has made his initial diagnosis, he can safely leave treatment in the hands of the nursing staff—and so it is with us. Only in a few instances is continued treatment by the doctor himself necessary, though the doctor (in our case the Selection and Treatment Committee) is kept in close touch with each man's progress, through my reports, and can continue to advise me from time to time.

The main difference in an otherwise fairly analogous position lies in this business of the transference. I (and my colleagues) have to effect a relationship with our "patients" of a kind far more delicate and difficult than the relationship of a nursing staff to their patients; a relationship far more fraught with dangerous possibilities, but one which, properly handled, can achieve great things. And when we have achieved the relationship we have so to conduct ourselves that it may in time be no longer necessary. When it is no longer necessary our work is done. Bryn now no longer needs to lean on Bods, though I imagine he will always have the warmest feelings towards him. So with Raymond and myself (to confine myself to the two cases of transference already mentioned). I cannot resist telling an interesting little story about Raymond. If you are sceptical about such things as symbolical stealing and all that is implied by them, this story should make you less so.

Raymond needed to feel quite certain that his love for me was returned—and that is a very difficult thing to prove, even if it is true. He was for the last year of his stay with us working in the office with me. He was learning shorthand and typing from my wife, and I used to dictate to him, for him to type, my non-confidential letters. Nearly every morning, before work could start, we used to have a conversation something like this:

RAYMOND: Can I have a pencil, please?

WILLS: But my dear boy, I gave you one yesterday morning—what have you done with it?

RAYMOND: No, you didn't.

WILLS: I'm quite sure I did.

RAYMOND: Don't be silly. Of course you didn't.

WILLS: Well, if I didn't, what pencil *were* you using yesterday?

RAYMOND: You didn't *give* me one, you lent me one, and I left it on your desk. . . .

Then a hunt would follow. The pencil never used to turn up, and Raymond would insist so vehemently that it was my fault that at last I would reluctantly find another one for him. Often, of course, I had no other to give him, and then he would say, "Oh well, I suppose I shall have to go and borrow one again. Only it's a bit thick, people are getting sick of having me come to borrow pencils from them." Then he would disappear for about twenty minutes, eventually returning with a pencil he claimed to have borrowed, but which I often remembered having once been in my possession. I (foolishly perhaps) never attached any particular importance to this. I thought the pencils were, each time, genuinely lost, and often used to accuse my wife of having pinched them, so that it was only in fun that I would sometimes say, "I believe you're stealing these pencils, and you've got an enormous hoard of them somewhere." Time passed, and the day came that Raymond was to leave. I had been slowly preparing him for the idea of being less dependent on me, but he had to leave somewhat before the period of his dependence was finished, because an opportunity offered itself that might not be repeated in a lifetime. The morning of his departure he came into the office with about thirty pencils, of all shapes, lengths and colours, from tiny bitten stubs to shiny full-length ones. "Here you are," he said, "I suppose you might as well have these back now." All these months, in order to re-assure himself, he had been stealing my love in the shape of its crudest symbol. Now he felt himself ready to get along without it.

One has to be continually on the look-out for little evidences like this, of how the land lies. It may be that the reason I did not recognize this beautiful little example (until its sequel) was that there was already ample other evidence in this case. But it was nevertheless a warning to me to keep a better look-out in future.

The importance of the transference, then, cannot be too highly stressed. It is odd that something which is really so well known needs to be stressed so heavily. Everyone knows that in war the company commander who can drag from his men that last extra inch of effort and sacrifice that makes the difference between victory and defeat is not the martinet. It is the captain that is loved by his men. I have never myself been a soldier, but all the evidence of war memoirs supports this belief. Indeed, no one but a dyed-in-the-wool martinet would deny it. Everyone knows that it is the schoolmaster who is loved that will get the most out of his boys. "Follow me," said Jesus of Nazareth to the simple fishermen, "and I will make you fishers of men." Was it the imperious glance, the commanding gesture, that made these poor workmen give up what little security they had to follow a vagabond preacher? Never! It was the love he was capable of inspiring that transformed these obscure men into apostles of the new message who were "turning the world upside down."

What love did then, love will do now. And yet the whole of our corrective machinery, whether the machinery of state justice or the simple machinery of family discipline, is carefully contrived to inspire as much as possible of a very different sentiment.

I wonder why?

CHAPTER TEN

Bunkers and Grousers

"I struck the board and cried 'No more!
I will abroad' "

GEO. HERBERT

MISS ETHEL MANNIN'S book *Rose and Sylvie* might have been written with Hawkspur Camp in mind, but for the fact that Miss Mannin had never heard of Hawkspur Camp when she wrote it. Except that it was co-educational, "Longmeadow Camp" might have been Hawkspur Camp, so faithfully are our method and regime reproduced. Hollyback, the Superintendent, even "copied" my trick of taking an inmate for a ride in the dilapidated old camp car (also faithfully reproduced) when he wanted to talk to him without interruption. But Hollyback has one habit for which I should take him to task if he really existed. Whenever any of his inmates become disgruntled he falls back on what seems to me an unfair and illogical argument. He says, "If you weren't here, you'd be somewhere much worse, with far less freedom, less sympathy, less hope for the future. You'd be 'disciplined' and given a rough time"—or words to that effect. I think it wrong to use that particular argument partly because it is not really the camp they are disgruntled with but themselves; and because if Hollyback and Miss Mannin and I had our way all such young people would be treated in some such place as Longmeadow Camp, and then we should have to get along without that particular argument.

But I have used it on occasion. I use it when someone who is on probation is thinking of bunking—I remind him that if he breaks the conditions of his probation the authorities might decide that Hawkspur Camp is a failure, and send him somewhere else—and somewhere worse.

I particularly remember using this argument with Willie Watson. Willie had an I.Q. of about 80 and was pretty hopeless. He was continually bunking and having to be fetched back from police stations in every direction. At last I pointed out to him very seriously that so far I had managed to keep his folly dark, but it couldn't be kept dark much longer, and when his Probation Officer found out about it, goodness knew what might happen. He bunked again, and then, everything else having failed, I fell back on threats. I said if it happened again I would report it to his Probation Officer, hinting darkly at what the consequences might be. After all, he had been sent to us instead of having three months' imprisonment, and if he refused this medicine, they might very well fall back on the other. He went again, so I kept my promise. On Sunday his Probation Officer, who was actually a very decent chap, came to the camp, gave Willie some cigarettes and a good talking to, and departed. The next day Willie was away again, and this time he smashed a shop window. He was arrested, and when I asked him at the police court why he had done it, he said "Well, you promised me that if I ran away again I could go to prison, and I ran away, but I didn't go to prison. They'll have to send me now." He was disappointed. They sent him to Borstal. And

I have no doubt that he is perfectly happy there. He had spent all his life in institutions of the old-fashioned type (which was why I couldn't just say "If you don't like it here buzz off home"—he had no home) and could not get along without the discipline of an authoritarian regime. I expect most of the rest of his life will be spent in institutions of one kind or another.

This story illustrates well the futility of threats, and it also shows that people may want to run away from a free and easy atmosphere like that of Hawkspur Camp.

Homer Lane tells us how the first inmates of the Little Commonwealth were sent there from London entirely without escort, saying, "They could not escape because there was no one to escape from." Homer Lane was the root and inspiration of all our work at Hawkspur Camp, but on this point I should take issue with him. I think he was very lucky that those young ladies got as far as Dorset. There *was* someone to run away from—there was themselves. I imagine Homer Lane discovered that before the Little Commonwealth was much older. Indeed, I think he must have known it all along, and was here indulging in that familiar little human weakness of sacrificing the true to the clever.

It is certainly something that I did not learn until after Hawkspur Camp had started. When I was in Borstal I used to say (though only to myself or my wife) "Of course the chaps 'scarper.' The walls and gates and constant locking and unlocking and counting of noses are a perpetual challenge and inducement." And so I still think they are. But I hereby offer my erstwhile employers, the Prison Commissioners, an unreserved apology for my disloyal thoughts, for I find there is very much more in it than that. We have no locks or walls or counting of noses at Hawkspur—but we have our fair share of running away.

I always say to a new arrival "If you don't like this place you're under no obligation, so far as I am concerned, to stay. Come and tell me, and I'll get into touch with your sponsors and ask them to make some other arrangements." Sometimes they took me at my word. I rarely attempted to dissuade them because as a rule they had changed their minds before I had had time to effect the formalities. Of course, one can generally tell when it is just a passing disgruntlement that is at the bottom of the wish to leave and in these cases I deliberately procrastinate writing to the sponsor, so that I shall not have the trouble of writing a countermanding letter in a day or two. I well remember the first case, when the camp had only been running about a month. Jim Payne wanted to leave. "Sure," I said, "there's no trouble about that. You'd be a fool to stay here if you don't like the place. I'll fix it up right away. But no—wait a minute though. Can you possibly hang on till Monday? I'm just off to catch the train for Birmingham to speak at a meeting there about the camp and I don't want to risk missing the train. If you could just manage to hang on till Monday it would be a great convenience to me. Then I'll make it my first job when I get back." Jim thought he could manage to last out over the week-end, so I said "Righto, thanks very much. Sorry to lose you though." Of course, when I came back on Monday Jim had forgotten all about leaving. I didn't know Jim very well then, but I got to know him pretty well during the ensuing two years and there is no doubt at all in my mind that if I had made the slightest attempt to dissuade him I shouldn't have found him there when I got back from my week-end.

But as a rule all this careful planning is of little avail, because there are many who do not want to *leave* so much as to run away. They feel themselves, vaguely or less vaguely, to be suffering from a desperate ill which calls for a desperate remedy, and running away—forcibly breaking the bonds—is much more desperate than merely "leaving."

What they are trying to run away from, of course, is their internal conflict—a conflict between two different sides of their nature, between their instinctive desires and the wishes of society or conscience. The worry and distress are so great that some way *must* be found of breaking away from them. "Perplexed and bewildered, Oh where shall I fly." Only a flight will do. The poet did not say "Perplexed and bewildered, Oh where shall I go?" And so a flight it often is.

I can often see it coming on, and then I try to find an opportunity of conveying to the boy concerned the fact that people often run away to try to escape from themselves, and how futile this is, and how it often brings worse misery. Not directly. To say it directly would be to kill it. They are trying to persuade themselves that I am part of what they are running away from, so anything I say against it is of little account. This is knowledge which they must acquire for themselves, but sometimes it is enough if they hear me saying it but without particular reference to themselves. So I have to keep eyes and ears open for an opportunity. It might happen like this. We are sitting round the fire in the day-room. The intending "bunker" is sitting hunched up in a corner, brooding, taking no notice of anyone or anything. Someone says, "How about a four for bridge?" and gets no answer, and a conversation might ensue like this:

WILLS: Not much enthusiasm for bridge since old Johnnie left.

A.: Oh, Johnnie—he could think of nothing else. Knew how to play, though.

WILLS: Remember how he used to lecture Ginger about what to bid and what not to bid?

B.: Funny the way old Ginger used to take it from him. He wouldn't take advice from anybody else about anything.

WILLS: Don't I know it.

A.: Why, did you try to give him some good advice then, Duke?

WILLS: Yes, I did depart from my rule on this occasion. It was when he was thinking of doing a bunk. (The prospective bunker probably pricks up his ears now, but I am looking anywhere but in his direction, and apparently do not even realize he is there.)

B.: I don't see why a chap shouldn't bunk if he wants to. Just like the Duke to poke his big nose in where it's not wanted.

WILLS: Of course, if *you* saw a chap stepping off the curb in front of a steam-roller you'd say "no business of mine," and walk on, wouldn't you?

B.: Sure I would. What's that to do with Ginger?

WILLS: Well, I don't mind anyone buzzing off that doesn't like it here. I sometimes wish a few of these grousers would make themselves scarce, without mentioning any names. But I knew perfectly well that Ginger was bunking for the same reason as most people bunk, and that he might not find out until it was too late to get back here.

B.: How do you mean? What d'you reckon he was bunking for then? Lot of tommy-rot I expect.

WILLS: Tommy-rot or not, they all discover I'm right sooner or later, only sometimes they don't find I was right till after they've bunked, that's why so many of them come back again.

A.: Well, come on then, cough it up—what is the Great Secret of Bunking?

WILLS: It's quite simple. They've got a lot of worries and things that get them all of a dither, and they want to get away from them. They kid themselves they're running away from the camp, but really they're trying to run away from themselves. Then when they get away they find they're just as fed up as before, so they think they might as well come back again, because the Duke was right for once.

B.: What a lot of boloney. Old Ginger didn't come back.

WILLS: (*quietly*) He couldn't. I knew he wouldn't be able to get back once he ran away, that's why I wasted good advice on him.

B.: Good old Ginger. Showed a bit of sense for once . . . and then the reminiscences drift elsewhere.

Sometimes that is enough, but when it is not, I have to decide whether to let it happen or not. If I had my way I would let it happen every time, and be ready to receive the absconder back when he had discovered the truth of my words. But there are often courts and policemen and probation officers to be considered, and it is not always feasible.

Mac was an interesting case in point. He had "run away" before coming to us. The youngest and least successful of a highly respectable suburban family, he had a long period of unemployment, and eventually absconded with a good sum of his mother's money and jewels. I need not here enter into the details of his conflicts, but he was an exceptionally nice person of about 23 or 24 years of age, liked and respected perhaps more than anyone in the camp. All the members went to Mac with their troubles, and yet he spent hours and hours brooding over his own. At last he said he couldn't stand it any longer, and must clear out. Now Mac was at the camp with a condition of residence from the Court, so it wasn't very simple. However I consulted with Dr. Carroll and we decided on a course of action. "All right," I said, "you don't like it here. You're fed up. Anywhere else would be better. You think you'd be all right in a job. O.K. then. I can't give you a job just by snapping my fingers, but we've arranged for you to leave the camp. You can go to London and live in a hostel until you've found a job, or one has been found for you. To-morrow." So to-morrow we saw him off in the bus, not noticing that he bought himself a return ticket! Shortly after eleven that night I had occasion to go into one of the bunk-houses—and there was Mac in bed!

And there, for a time, the matter rested. But soon Mac began to work up again. We got him one or two jobs because he was still anxious to leave, and the camp was doing him very little good while he was in that frame of mind. But he threw them up, or got himself sacked, in the most prodigal way, always returning to the camp. I began to hope that soon he would realize that it was himself and not the camp he was trying to run away from, and indeed I think he was getting near it. But then he conceived another idea. It was not that he wanted to get away from the camp, but that he wanted to go *home*—then he would be happy, and all would be well. This his Probation Officer would not agree to, so Mac said, "Permission or none, I'm going. I'm going on September 15th, whether Mr. Steady (Probation Officer) likes it or not." "You're a chump," I said. "Have you told Brother Steady about this?" "Yes. I wrote him yesterday." So I promptly wrote to Steady myself, and urged him to let Mac go—to send him his fare, indeed. Or, if he must take a strong line, not to say anything harsher than "If you do come home you'll only be packed off to the camp again." But Mr. Steady, although he was one of the best of the many Probation Officers who have had dealings with Hawkspur camp, could not see eye to eye with me about this—probably for perfectly good and sufficient reasons of is own. He wrote instead a very stern, denunciatory letter to Mac, reminding him that an abscondence from the camp would be a breach of his Probation Order, and therefore a criminal offence. If Mac committed this offence, Mr. Steady would waste no more time on him but would have him hauled before the Court with a strong recommendation (which he had not the slightest doubt would be accepted) that Mac be sent to Borstal. But Mac was not to be deterred by that. He was inclined to suspect that this was an empty threat (although Mr. Steady had assured both him and me that it was not), but even if it were not, he was so certain that at home he would find peace that he was prepared to run the risk. Or would it be more true to say he was so anxious to determine once and for all whether it really *was* himself he was running away from that no price seemed too high to pay for certainty? Anyway, he was determined to go, and I had very little doubt that he *would* go. But on the 14th of September—the day before the ultimatum expired—Mr. Steady arrived at the camp and took Mac away for a week's holiday. So the fateful day was tided over, and Mac never made his test. He had screwed his courage up to the necessary point once, and Mr. Steady rightly assumed that he would never be able to screw it up again.

Eventually circumstances made it possible for me to demand that Mac be received home, though I could no longer offer to have him back if he wanted to come. The war, which began after I had started writing this book, has made it impossible to judge how Mac is really progressing now, as he is in the abnormal environment of the Army. He was a very difficult case, and really ought to have had psychotherapy but he was unfortunately unsuitable for this type of treatment, for reasons which need not be gone into here. But I feel fairly certain that if my good friend Mr. Steady had allowed him to bunk when he wanted to, we might have had better results.

I seem to be suggesting that everyone who runs away is running away from himself. Of course that is not the case, though I dare venture to guess that it is much more often the cause than is commonly supposed. I cannot presume to make a catalogue of all possible reasons for absconding, but there is one other major cause, and unfortunately the treatment called for in this case is just the opposite from what is called for in the other. Boys whose chief need is for that sense of security that can only come from an assurance that one is loved often behave badly in order to test their security—in order to see whether the person from whom one is demanding affection can be put off by misbehaviour, or whether the security is absolute. I have given examples of this elsewhere. Less commonly, I think, persons of this type adopt another expedient—they run away, or threaten to run away in order to see whether the person whose love they need will pursue them, or entreat them not to go. It would be an unqualified disaster to such a person if (in the case of the camp) I were just to say "Righto. Good-bye." That would confirm their worst fears and create great unrest. I have therefore spent many hours "wrestling" with such persons, of whom the most outstanding was perhaps Raymond. During his first six months at the camp Raymond seemed to be perfectly happy, though it could not be said that he was "getting anywhere." He was inoffensive, irresponsible, and idle, and that was all. But he was growing up (he was sixteen when he came to us) and after a time we noticed a change. I need not go into details except to say that this was about the time he began to make a very strong positive transference to me, and he needed very intensely to feel that his affection was returned. This was the beginning of his "cure" (though not by any means the whole of it), though it put an end for the time being to his carefree happiness. He began to say he could stand the place no longer, and must get away at all costs, though he had no home to speak of, detested his father, and had no idea where he could go if he did leave. If he had not been so happy during his first few months I should have felt that he had pretty solid grounds for feeling miserable. He had a sensitive, highly strung disposition, and I had been surprised how well he was standing up to the roughness and crudities of camp life. It was difficult to find an adequate reply to some of his complaints, many of which had a solid enough basis. But (although I did not harp on this when talking to him) it was a great help to me to remember how easily he had endured the camp at first—when, indeed, it had been much cruder. He would come to me feeling absolutely desperate. I do not mean pretending, or merely appearing, desperate. He really did feel desperate, and our talks were apt to be tense and portentous. Each time he felt that he had positively reached the end of his tether, and must go. Each time I tried to reply to all his arguments, and at the same time, directly or indirectly, tell him how much I personally wanted him to stay. He would leave me feeling somewhat relieved, but never admitting it, until the next storm blew up in a week or two's time. I did all manner of things to make the camp easier for him, by way of demonstration of my desire to keep him, often causing acute jealousy. Eventually another boy struck him, somewhat viciously, and he went ("Wills cannot really love me or he would not want me to stay in a place where I can be subjected to such things as this"). I went after him, post-haste, in the car. I overtook him before he reached the village, and took him into my house there, where I spent a very long time fighting his adamantine determination to run away. He continued to resist long after he had actually given up the idea, and I, though I knew he would not now go, continued to fight his resistance, because every argument I used was an additional buttress to his belief that perhaps I did love him after all.

Even so, there was in Raymond's running away a considerable element of the other reason—running away from one's self—and in talking to him one had to phrase every remark very carefully to take each of these two elements into consideration.

What I have said about escaping from one's mental conflict applies equally to the grousers as to the bunkers. There is plenty to grouse about at Hawkspur Camp in all conscience. But it is both exasperating and amusing to see *who* grouses at *what*. And it is extremely instructive.

Daniel Womack asked me to call a special meeting of the Camp Council before he had been with us a week, because he had something very important to discuss. We held the meeting. Daniel said the place was filthy, it stank, it was a bloody disgrace, it wasn't fit for pigs to live in. All that was needed was soap, water, and a little elbow grease, and he was calling for volunteers. He was howled down, partly because it wasn't as bad as all that, and partly because it was considered unbecoming for a newcomer to cast reflections on our conduct prior to his arrival. But before many days had passed we discovered something which would have given us far better reason for howling him down. We found that if there was one thing in the camp that needed a good scrubbing more than any other, that thing was Daniel Womack!

Tom Beeley who, when he came to us, but not now, was spineless, weak-kneed, shiftless, and entirely without self-discipline was always complaining about the lack of discipline in the camp. T. Miner was a Welshman with the mercurial temperament of the Welsh. He had violent but short-lived enthusiasms and his chief grouse was that "things in this adjectival place get started, but never adverbially finished."

These people of course are just projecting (as the psychologists say) their own particular failings on to their environment. But there are also those who are chronically dissatisfied with themselves and who project their general disgruntlement on to the camp in general, and grouse about every mortal thing. Reggie Male was an admirable example of this. He was profoundly dissatisfied with himself and attempted to compensate his dissatisfaction by exaggerated imagining of his exploits. He had done wonderful things in the past (we were given to understand) and even now he could do most things better than anyone in the camp. This attitude used to make him unpopular, and his popularity was not increased by the fact that while some of his tales he told us must have been untrue, there was no doubting his competence and efficiency at the camp. But he won back some small share of popularity by his consistent and unwavering attitude of mild cynicism about everything and everyone at the camp. Everything was always wrong, and Reggie always knew the remedy. He was very intelligent and his carping and grousing did a great deal to undermine morale. One could only wait and hope that the various influences brought to bear on him at the camp would eventually increase his opinion of himself and thus of everyone else. In the case of Reggie there was a particular sign for which I looked, which would tell me that he was well on his way. Many of the exploits about which he told us were connected with cars. I happened to know that he had failed his driving test and therefore had done very little driving indeed. I felt that when the time came that he no longer needed to boast about his skill as a driver, and was prepared to admit that in fact he had no driving licence, we should be able to feel that he was making real progress. When he seemed much better we sent him to a job with a friend of mine, but I still felt a little dubious because he still had not reached the point I had set for him in my mind. After about a year his usefulness with my friend came to an end, and it was arranged that he should leave, though without any feeling that he was being "sacked." Instead of going home, he came back to the camp, about which he used to grouse so much, because he said he knew that we alone could give him what he needed. Very soon after his return he began to take an entirely different attitude to this question of driving skill, and even admitted to me that he had no driving licence. A little while later he admitted it to the camp in general (by implication, of course, not by some kind of general confession) and for over a year now he has been doing a very useful piece of work in connection with evacuee children.

I end this weary catalogue of grousers with an interesting example of both grousing and bunking. Cuthbert Parsons had completely repressed his homosexual leanings so that, while he was quite unaware of any conflict, his repressed desires found expression in ways which, while never homosexual, and often quite innocuous, did sometimes land him in trouble. At the camp he began by being loyal and helpful, someone who could always be relied on to do the right thing or speak a word in season with his fellow-members. He started a course of psychotherapy, and as the psychotherapist began to touch the hidden springs of the anti-social acts which had brought him to us, so his conflicts were brought a little nearer consciousness. Then—and not until then—he became a furtive grouser, complaining about me and everything at the camp behind my back, while remaining perfectly loyal on the surface. This gradually became worse until eventually he could stand it no longer and absconded—taking some of my money with him. It was thus clear to me that, although he was running away from the camp (in an effort to escape himself), he was also anxious to retain it—and therefore took a small part of it with him. So I expected him back, and in due course back he came. A second time he went through exactly the same cycle, except that this time he did not, so far as I know, steal anything when he left. A third time he came back—having walked a hundred miles to do so. But this time his sponsors were tired of him and would pay no more, and he declined psychotherapy, without which we could not hope to help him. A friend offered him a job, which he took, and we parted company. I do not know what has happened to him, but I fear the prognosis is not very favourable. Dr. Denis Carroll of the Institute for the Scientific Treatment of Delinquency tells me that this is no uncommon occurrence in the psychological treatment of delinquency. The symptoms of the "disease" from which the delinquent suffers are not as painful as those endured by the neurotic, and he is therefore not always anxious for a cure if it is a difficult process. So just as the psychotherapist begins to feel that he is getting somewhere the patient finds he "can't take it" and fails to turn up for treatment. But Dr. Carroll and his colleagues are not discouraged by this. Apparently they all come back sooner or later, though often they have been to prison in the meantime. And so with our bunkers—they're sure to come back if they need us—and if they can. So we are not alarmed or discouraged by grousings and grumblings and runnings away—they are just the expected symptoms of what we are trying to cure.

Anyway, we've always got Willie Cook, our most spectacular cure, to cheer us up, though I hope you will not take this as seriously as the old lady who asked me whether I *really* thought we had cured Willie in one day. Willie had been ill, and after a more than adequate period of convalescence refused to go to work. So a social worker in London asked me if we would try him at the camp. He came one autumn evening, while we were having our Harvest Supper. Next morning he took one good look at the camp, went back to the social worker in London and asked her to find him a job!

CHAPTER ELEVEN

Sex

"Now I don't want any coarse remarks"
PLATO'S SYMPOSIUM (ACC. JOYCE)

THERE are no lewd drawings on the walls of the latrines at Hawkspur Camp. Our wooden buildings—some of them unpainted inside—have many square yards of excellent drawing surface, but in three and a half years only one piece of obscenity has appeared. I should be neither shocked nor worried if it did appear. But I find it very interesting that, in fact, it does not.

The reason is that sex is not a shameful secret at Hawkspur Camp. It is discussed openly and, when the novelty wears off, unaffectedly. There is no giggling or "hushing" when in the course of a discussion someone says he can't get to sleep unless he masturbates first. A mental note is made of the statement by any Staff member who happens to hear it, but there is neither reproach nor reprimand. On the contrary, we feel that progress is being made if a boy doesn't deny doing what in fact every normal person *does* do at one time or another. In connection with that particular remark I am reminded of an interesting side issue. We had a visit from the schoolmaster and probation officer of the boy who made it. They asked me about masturbation. I said that masturbation was one of his difficulties. I said this not merely on the evidence of the remarks I have quoted, but because he had talked to me about it a good deal. He had been told with a good deal of authority that the seminal fluid was grey matter, and every time he masturbated successfully he lost some of his brain via the spinal column. He was afraid to talk about it at first, but when he discovered I really did not condemn masturbation he came out with it.

So I said, "Yes, masturbation was one of his difficulties." I thought I was dealing with fairly sensible people. A little later on they saw him, alone, and in a tone of horror accused him of the shocking vice of self-abuse. Of course he just denied it vehemently and further blackened himself in their eyes by adding the sin of lying to the wickedness of "impurity." I just mention this to show how absolutely impossible it is ever to hope to establish a *rapport* from which therapy can begin if one starts with an attitude of moral superiority and condemnation. I suppose there is still a slight difference of opinion in enlightened circles about the physical effect of masturbation. But there can be no doubt that guilt and fear arising from these fantastic stories about the effects of masturbation do definitely more harm to the psyche than is ever done to the body by the act of masturbation itself.

Masturbation is a problem that causes me a great deal of trouble and effort. Not in trying to get people to stop masturbating. Even I do not attempt the impossible. But in trying to get the poor victim really to believe that his bit of regular masturbation will not diminish the quantity of his brain, will not make him weak and infertile, will not make him a nervous wreck, will not send him mad, will not make his hair and finger-nails fall out, and that it is not a frightful, shocking sin for which he merits eternal damnation, and that it is not a filthy, beastly habit which makes him unfit for the company of a "pure" girl. I tell them that the "pure" girl probably masturbates as much as he does, and I personally should think none the less of her for doing it. But, alas, it takes a long time to overcome the pernicious influence of ignorant parents, teachers, probation officers, parsons, and even, if I am to believe what they tell me, doctors. That is all I do about masturbation *per se*. If I can get them to get rid of their ridiculous fear and shame and guilt about this very ordinary habit, I say no more about it.

Masturbation is a vicious circle. It creates a feeling of shame, which drives the victim in upon himself, and leads to further masturbation. So get rid of the shame! If I can do something towards that, I feel I can safely leave the rest to Hawkspur Camp. When he learns to mix with other people in a healthy, co-operative way, and no longer feels that he is an unloved outcast, and has found outlets for his interests and energy—well, I don't think masturbation will worry him enough for it to worry me!

One young man took up a piece of paper one day and drew on it an enormous penis, with a good deal of detail. This was during a "handwork" session, and he showed it to my colleague, Walter Smith. Walter Smith examined it appraisingly and expressed an opinion on it as a drawing, just as if it had been a drawing of a vase of chrysanthemums or a bowl of fruit, and handed it back. Dick then set to work on it again, and in a few deft strokes converted it into something quite different. Dick was not highly intelligent and Walter praised him for his clever work. Further, he encouraged him to do the same thing again, and Dick spent many handwork sessions doing just that. By and by he exhausted his interest in drawing penises and went on to "straight" drawing, from which he derived a good deal of satisfaction.

Dick had a great deal of inferiority feeling about his sexual organs, and I am sure Walter Smith helped him to get rid of at least some of it. His story is an interesting one. I tell it as he told it to me. Whether it is true or not does not matter. Its meaning, for him, and for me, is the same whether it is history or phantasy. Walking in the park one day with a friend they saw a policemen "move on" some courting couples, and the friend said "what fun—we could do that." So pretending to be a pair of plain clothes policemen they "moved on" some lovers themselves. Dick then tried it by himself, but whereas the man obeyed him, the woman challenged him to prove that he was a policeman. "Ho," says Dick, "you don't believe me, then? Well, it happens that I haven't got my badge with me, but if you'll come with me to the telephone box I'll soon show you." The girl called his bluff and went with him. He 'phoned the police station and asked them to send a car to pull in a woman he had caught in the act of indecent behaviour in public. The police sent a car—and pulled in our Dick. So whether the story is true or not, there is clear evidence of a desire to show superiority over persons engaging in sexual activity, in order to compensate his own feeling of inferiority in that sphere. When he came to the camp he told everyone that he had the biggest "tool" in the city from which he came—another piece of compensatory phantasy.

Only psychotherapy can deal adequately with a thing of this kind, and Dick is not considered "bright" enough for that, so we have had to manage without. Closely connected in his mind with the sexual inferiority (perhaps at the root of it) are the dreadful acne scars with which his face is pitted. He says if only he could get rid of his scars he would get married. Acne is not an easy thing to get rid of, but our Hon. Medical Officer is doing the best he can with injections. Perhaps it will do the trick. But how perfectly futile to be shocked by this unhappy lad or to tell him he's "wicked" or "impure" and ought to be punished. He is no more guilty than a child who catches diphtheria, and much less blameworthy than an adult who catches a cold!

The whole trouble is that our parents were ashamed of the way they begat us and have never been able to talk to us about it without embarrassment. Not all go to the length of the scoutmaster in a previous chapter who said "it's nasty but it's necessary." The nastiness is implied rather than expressed by the horror with which perfectly natural exploration or exhibitionism is forbidden to youngsters. If there is any real guilt in the parents' mind about the question of sex this embarrassment is of course intensified.

We had at the camp a very charming youth of twenty-one who was born out of wedlock. After he was born his mother, who was apparently a very nice as well as an attractive woman, met a "steadier" young man who married her and accepted complete responsibility for Bryn. He promised her that he would be in every sense a real father to Bryn, and through many years he kept his promise. Whatever disadvantages may accrue from having a step-father they were certainly not due in this case to any failings in the "father." I once asked Edward Bawden why he did not allow me to drive him back from London, as we both returned on the same evening and he had no car. He said it was certainly not because he wanted to prevent anyone from doing a kindness—he never did that because it gives the doer so much pleasure. That element may have been present with Bryn's father. Every time he set eyes on Bryn he was reminded of his virtue in this voluntary adoption of the offspring of his wife's frailty. Bryn therefore found favour in his step-father's eyes and their happy relationship flowered. But if his step-father found in Bryn a symbol of his own virtue, it was quite otherwise that his mother viewed him. Running about the home, playing with her husband and her later children, growing slowly to manhood, she watched with deep distrust the tangible evidence of her own folly, sin, and weakness. Every kindness shown to Bryn by her husband seemed like a fresh condonation of her guilt. And like the rest of us, she didn't want her guilt condoned—she wanted it punished. Bryn could not fail to be conscious of this distrust and fear and dislike, if only because of the contrast with his father's attitude. The effect of thus being deprived of a mother's affection are dealt with elsewhere, and they were not lacking in Bryn's case. What I am concerned with now is his sexual development. To Bryn's mother, sex was inextricably associated with a guilty secret of which he was in a very real sense the very personification. Is it to be expected that she could be calm and rational in her attitude to sex with Bryn? Between his mother's horror of sex and his father's condonation of human frailty (for he knew all about himself by now) Bryn's attitude to the question beggars description. After he had come to us a girl in his mother's town accused him of being the father of her bastard, but when he denied it decided not to go to court. The mere suspicion, however, was enough for Bryn's mother. To her bastard son she sent a letter, angry, bitter, reproachful, full of vituperation, for having committed the same offence with which she brought him into the world. At last her punishment had come upon her, and upon Bryn she could shower all the reproaches that she herself had earned but had been denied. In punishing Bryn she was punishing herself. Bryn's suspected sinfulness opened the floodgates which released the murky waters which, and this is the important point, had been there all the time, and had seeped through at a thousand points to colour her relationship to Bryn and thus his relationship to sex and to the world. There is embarrassment, there is guilt, and of course there is a certain jealousy about the possession of this particular piece of knowledge. Tell the brats all about it and they'll know as much as we do—and where's our authority then? I am not going to say that parents actually argue in that way, but there is certainly something of that feeling behind it all.

So between embarrassment, guilt, and jealousy, the parent, does his best to keep his (and of course her) child in ignorance. This fruit being forbidden becomes more tempting, as it did to God's children in the Garden of Eden. The locked door is the one that *must* be opened, and like Bluebeard's wife, we are often disappointed when we force our way in. Like her, too, we are filled with fear and forboding about the things we discover, and it is associated in our minds not with all the intense joy and satisfaction that a good sexual relationship can provide but with furtiveness, with fear of discovery, with fear of all manner of evil consequences.

Sometimes to the other difficulties is added another factor tending to keep the child in ignorance. That is the very common reluctance of parents to admit that their child is really grown up. This may be due to a number of causes. Chiefly it is due to the unhappy implications of having a grown-up son or daughter—when he is grown up I shall be on the down grade, and he in the prime of his strength. I shall be getting weaker and middle-aged spread when she is entering the full bloom of her youth. This evil day must be fended off, and it is done by deceiving ourselves that our offspring are still children.

How well I remember Willie Jukes. He couldn't go anywhere without his mother, and when he left school he wouldn't go to work because going to work separated him from mother. Once I had met the mother and talked to her about Willie, I had no further need to wonder how this had come about. By the time Willie was twenty-one, Mrs. Jukes was able to deceive herself no longer, and tried to find some way to mitigate the effects of her folly. So Willie came to Hawkspur. Although Mrs. Jukes wanted Willie to "grow up," neither she nor her husband had ever said anything to him about sex, except to describe the horrible things that happen to little boys who "play about with themselves." When he came to us Willie knew that he could effect a most exciting and agreeable sensation by a certain manipulation of his penis. But he was frightfully worried about it because every time he did it some brains came out. At twenty-one years of age he did not know where babies came from. He simply did not know anything about it.

I took him for a ride in the car and told him quite brutally "the facts of life." He was intensely interested, but I believe he thought I was a very nasty man as well as an awful liar. Whenever I paused in my narrative he urged me to continue. But he did it symbolically. He asked me some question about the inside mechanism of the car! I don't know that this story is particularly instructive except as a solemn warning to parents. We couldn't do anything for Willie. After about three weeks he went home to Mummy—walked fifty miles to London—and Mummy of course received him with open arms and said dear Willie shouldn't go back to that nasty camp any more. What has happened to him now I don't know.

I am sometimes asked why the camp is not co-educational. I think perhaps the answer is that what we are concerned with is not education but re-education, and co-re-education is a very different proposition from co-education. In co-education you have more or less normal children learning to acquire a normal and healthy relationship to each other. For all practical purposes the children, when they start school, haven't got any attitude to each other and it is the job of the co-educator to see that they get one. In our re-education we have not children but young adults (at any rate physically) who have got an attitude to girls and a deplorable one it is. If we were co-educational we should have young women with an equally deplorable attitude to the other sex. The free atmosphere of Hawkspur Camp is no guarantee against their giving expression to their unfortunate attitude to each other, and while I think there is less likelihood of "accident" in our atmosphere than in the atmosphere in which they were brought up, I don't care to run the risk.

But that is not to say that the boys at Hawkspur Camp never see any girls. They are quite free at all times to fraternize (if that is the right word) with the village girls, and if I find a boy is getting "thick" with a girl I always try to persuade him to bring her up to the camp to tea sometime—but in this I have not often been successful. Then, too, we have our socials from time to time, and some of them are open to the "public," which generally means two or three families in our immediate neighbourhood. Although naturally there is a fair amount of good-natured leg-pulling about it, I always try to take the line that having a girl friend is a perfectly natural state of affairs. That is quite new to them. Their parents having the kind of attitude I have already referred to, regard any sign of intimacy with girls with suspicion. They are never more pleased than if they can say, "Oh yes, Johnnie's a very good boy. He takes no interest in girls." This reminds me of a grocer I know who was talking about his dog. It was a question of the paternity of a mongrel pup I had bought. Mr. Grocer didn't think *his* dog could be the father. "No Mr. Wills," he said with a perfectly serious face, "I never see him sniffing round a lady dog. He's a very pure dog really." As Mr. Grocer obviously does not consider himself a pure man, what chance is there of his daughter growing up a pure woman—in any real sense?

In spite of the perfect freedom in this respect at Hawkspur Camp—or should I say because of this freedom?—we have never had, if I may be forgiven the euphemism, any "trouble." At least we have only once had any trouble and that was when the vicar, much disturbed, came to me to complain that my young men had been keeping some girls out late at night. I forebore, with some difficulty, from the obvious *tu quoque* that his village girls had caused me much inconvenience by keeping my boys out late, and read the boys concerned a lecture on the stupidity of getting themselves "in dutch" with the villagers, which had more or less the desired effect.

One winter's night two of the younger members of the camp followed the Lothario of that time, to see what happens when one takes a girl out. We listened hilariously in the day-room to the story of how he had gone down to the village and, standing outside the place where his girl was employed as a servant girl, had taken out his handkerchief and blown two tremendous blasts on his nose as a signal of his presence. Shortly after this the young lady emerged and they walked half a mile along the road to an old barn, which they entered, the two peeping Toms not far behind them. Lothario and his girl settled themselves down in a corner and the other two crept as near as they dare. There was some desultory conversation, and then there started what was apparently a nightly ritual. Lothario began to sing. His singing voice was one of the standing jokes of the camp and here he was singing to his girl! But after all, he only knows about a hero from the movies, and the hero there often sings to the heroine. After the song the hero usually kisses the heroine, and our hero did the same. They never go any further than that on the movies, so neither did our hero. He had been singing cowboy songs—*Old Faithful*, and what not—but when she said in a tender whisper "You're *my* cowboy," our two young friends ran shrieking from the barn. Such are the innocent sexual diversions of the more daring of our Romeos, but such affairs are few and far between.

I have spoken elsewhere of Tom Beeley, whose father said he was good for nothing. He was, in his day, our chief Lothario, though not the singing cowboy referred to above. He had lots of girls, but he was never able to stick to one for very long because he could never escape the conviction that in keeping company with a girl he was doing something he ought not to do. This inconstancy of course only exacerbated his father's annoyance, and he was soundly rated for going about not only with a girl, which was, he was allowed to gather, bad enough, but for going about with so many. He came to Hawkspur Camp and began to be conscious of a difference in the atmosphere about this question. He told the most astounding stories about his sexual exploits to the fellows in the bunk-house and at the same time very furtively, very surreptitiously he began to make the acquaintance of the local girls. I soon heard all about this because the chaps in whom he confided realized, as he didn't, that there was no earthly reason to keep it secret from the Duke. And of course I casually alluded to it from time to time, enquired whether the girl was anyone I knew, and so on. Presently, however, a really serious affair began to blow up. A girl from London came to spend her holidays with a neighbouring farmer. Tom fell for her, and they spent many hours together. She returned to London. Tom was inconsolable, and one week-end disappeared. After a few days he returned and I gave him a good telling-off. I had not, I assured him, the slightest objection to his clearing off when and where he liked, but I did think I was entitled to the elementary courtesy of being informed of his whereabouts. Apart from anything else, it was my duty to report disappearances to the probation officer concerned. If someone clears off like that, how am I to know it is just a week-end off and not a bunk? On this occasion, fortunately for Tom, I had assumed it to be what in fact it was, and asked him why he hadn't told me about it. He was quite frank. He said he was in love. The object of his affections was in London, fifty miles away, and he had hitch-hiked to see her. "What's wrong with that?" he asked belligerently, feeling in his heart of hearts that there must be something very wrong with it somewhere, because it would have made his father very angry. I replied that there was only one thing that was wrong with it, its extreme furtiveness. Otherwise it was the most natural thing in the world. I hoped he'd had a good time and I hoped he'd tell me before I went next time. It was very difficult for him to believe there was not a catch somewhere in all this. Two or three weeks later he put me to the test. "I suppose it'll be all right for me to go and see my girl this week-end?" he said.

"Sure, sure," I said. "Thanks for letting me know. Back Monday?"

"Yes."

"O.K. then."

He hesitated. There was apparently something else he wanted to say—"er . . . you send reports to Mr. Downcast, don't you?" (Mr. Downcast was his P.O.)

"Yes, I have to send a report to Mr. Downcast each month. I tell him just as much as I think is good for him. Why?"

"Er . . . well, if you tell him about this he'll tell my father and then I shall get into a row."

"What, for just seeing a girl? . . . Isn't your old man human then?"

But it appeared that it wasn't merely the girl. It was also the business of hitch-hiking which would have horrified his highly-respectable father. I didn't want to keep the P.O. in complete ignorance of this girl business just in case something went wrong somewhere and it all came out afterwards. So I put forward a plan. My plan was that he should not go up this week-end, but should come in the car with me on Tuesday, and I would meet him and his girl and take them to tea somewhere. Of course I knew what a nice girl she was because he had told me. But if I saw her myself I could tell Mr. Downcast that I had seen her and thoroughly approved of her. And then I would arrange for Tom to spend a week-end in London every four or five weeks at my expense. He was quite astounded by all this, and while regretting missing the ensuing week-end he fell in readily with my plan.

The following Tuesday I took them out to tea. I took them to the Curb Café near Charing Cross Station because I thought its sybaritic furnishings would suit his mood. She was a nice girl, a clerk, and she assured me that she was aware of all Tommie's shortcomings, that she was prepared to wait till he was able to marry her and then stand by him in his weaknesses. Tom looked down his nose, and said something to the effect that with a prize like her before him he was not likely to stray from the path of rectitude.

So we had a very nice party, and then we all went home, and I promised Tom his monthly visit.

I never had to pay for a single visit. I had given him what he wanted, which was not, primarily at that time, a girl. He wanted reassurance. He wanted to have it proved to him that I really did approve of him and considered him fit to associate with girls; that I really did believe that having a girl was a perfectly natural and desirable thing, and that I really was prepared to take his side against his parents.

Thus fortified and reassured he left Hawkspur Camp in due course, took up with one of his old "flames" and in defiance of his father's anger, married her, and has lived happily ever after. But observe the side issue. He is able to support a wife, yet I am quite sure his father was right before, when he said he wasn't. While the conflicts about sex were unresolved he had no energy to spare for anything else; he was idle, feckless, irresponsible. While he was with us he settled his sexual problem and when he left there was such a change in his character that when he lost a job, he was not content just to go on the dole and do nothing, he preferred to eke out a precarious but industrious existence at jobbing gardening, so that a meed of praise was forced even from the reluctant lips of his father.

I can imagine some of my readers asking themselves whether Wills thinks that sex is the cause of everything. What I have been trying to convey here is that it isn't sex but people's ignorance and stupidity about sex that causes so much misery and frustration and delinquency. If only we can learn to talk about copulation as naturally as we talk about digestion we shall have gone a long way to making a world fit for children to be brought up in. "The day is coming," says W. N. P. Barbellion in his *Journal of a Disappointed Man*, "when a joke about sex will be not so much objectionable as unintelligible." I see little evidence that he was right. I wish he were.

CHAPTER TWELVE

Homosexuality

"and the moral of that is—
'Be what you would seem to be'"
"ALICE IN WONDERLAND"

VISITORS sometimes say "What about sex?" and looking at me in what can only be described as "a certain manner" say, "Do you ever have any trouble with the boys in the bunk-houses?" By which I gather them to be enquiring about homosexuality. In the sense in which these enquirers mean it we have had no trouble about homosexuality. It is true that we had a young man who used to get up in the middle of the night and go round from bunk to bunk, asking the occupants to move over because he had an erection he wanted to get rid of, but he was just regarded as a harmless nuisance, and was told, not too politely, to go back to bed. This lad is an interesting commentary on our penal system. He had enjoyed all the grades of "treatment" available up to, but not including, a convict prison. His education started at an approved school. In due course he found himself in Borstal, and later had several sentences of imprisonment. A discriminating social worker in his native town penetrated to the innate childlikeness and gentleness beneath his tough crust and thought perhaps we might be able to liquidate the crust and bring out the real man—although normally we do not take such experienced people. Now, as I have said elsewhere, no human institution can be expected to achieve perfection and I—as I know something of their difficulties—should be the last to expect it of our corrective institutions. But here was a man of twenty-three who had spent most of his life in corrective institutions, at each of which he was, presumably, under the surveillance of a paid medical officer. It was not, however, until he reached Hawkspur Camp that it was discovered that he was suffering from the after effects of Encephalitis Lethargica. Most people now know, I suppose, that Encephalitis Lethargica (sleepy sickness) is often followed by —among other things—a kind of moral obliquity, which the patient is quite unable to control. This boy suffered repeated punishment because he had been ill. He is now in a mental hospital, which is, alas, the only place for such people at present.

It is true also that we had a young man of very limited intelligence who offered—quite openly and publicly—to take his trousers down for anyone for a couple of cigarettes, though the Staff were offered the privilege without fee. He too was regarded as a harmless nuisance. He, too—though for different reasons—will probably have to spend his days in an institution of some kind. But apart from these two grossly abnormal people there has been no homosexuality at the camp—in the sense in which the enquirers mean it. But that is not to say we have had no homosexuals.

Edward is typical of the way in which we have come up against this problem. He came from an ordinary "superior" working-class family, living in a suburb of London. Outside his work the father's chief interest was the League tables. The mother's horizon was bounded by the walls of her home.

Gertie was an ordinary sort of girl who worked behind a counter somewhere. Edward, however, from about the time he left school, began to be rather different from the others. He seemed highly strung, nervous, and a trifle irritable. "There must be something wrong with him," his father said to me, "or he wouldn't want to spend hours and hours listening to that highbrow music." There was something "wrong" with him, though to this day I have never dared to tell his father what it is. He knew himself there was "something wrong." He saw, as he developed towards puberty, that other lads ran around with girls, some frivolously, some seriously, but all apparently getting a good deal of satisfaction from it. He, however, never had any desire to mix with girls and this in itself was disturbing. What was more disturbing was that he found himself growing extremely fond of other fellows, sometimes being strongly—even thrillingly—stirred when they touched him. This fact in itself would not have upset him unduly if it had not been that his friends experienced no reciprocal feelings toward him, though he gathered from their talk that they did have such feelings in connection with girls. The conviction slowly grew upon him that he was "abnormal." He began tentatively one day to talk about it to his mother, but she, horrified at the trend of the conversation, passed him on to his father. Father, disgusted beyond measure, said there was to be no more of this nonsense, and that was that. "What have I done wrong?" said Edward to himself, and began to try to find out. He could find out very little. All references to men being fond of each other were occasions either for giggling or indignant disgust. He began to feel more and more an outcast, he had a constant sense of shame and guilt, coupled with a fierce resentment at the society which created these feelings in him, but gave him no explanation of them. He became moody and introspective, spent hours brooding, was late for work and generally a worry to his mother and to himself. Presently the conflict between his perfectly natural inclination and the demands of society became so intense that it precluded other activities, he was unable to concentrate on anything, gave up his job, and eventually came to Hawkspur Camp.

Hawkspur Camp suited him because we made no demands on him, didn't nag him when he brooded and were not shocked when he began—very, very tentatively—to steer the conversation towards the problem that was tormenting him. From the first we put him in the hands of a psychotherapist. And at this point it might be wise for me to insert a "saving clause." Homosexuality was not the whole of Edward's trouble, and if here or in any other instance I have quoted throughout the book I seem to be over-simplifying the problem, this is only for the sake of clarity, and not because, in actual fact, the other aspects were ignored. I have no doubt that the psychotherapist dealt with the question of homosexuality among other things, but the circumstances were such that the psychotherapy was bound to be superficial, and while general stability might be increased, it is doubtful whether he could be made quite "normal" whatever that may mean. Edward in time, as he learned that we were different from his parents, came to talk freely about his inversion. He wanted to know if it was "wrong" to feel like that, and I said of course it isn't. I told him I knew several very fine men who feel just as he does, and some of them could be reckoned among the salt of the earth. I explained how some men with this capacity for loving their fellows turn it to good account by doing splendid work as boys' club leaders, and so on; of how others "sublimated" a good deal of their sexual energy into artistic channels; of how, more often than not, the homosexual was a more than usually sensitive and refined person. It took him a long time to believe that this could really be true, eager as he was to believe it. I gave him books to read and he himself got hold of the short edition of Havelock Ellis's *Psychology of Sex*.

Many may condemn me for this attitude. They will say that I am only making Edward more introspective, and I should try to get him to think of other things. The answer is simple—and it is Edward's answer—"I can't concentrate on anything." He must first resolve this conflict.

"What is to happen to me?" he would say. "Must I always be like this?" I said there are three possible outcomes. One is that the "Uranism" is just a phase, such as we all go through, though many of us do not even notice it, and that he would grow out of it. The second possibility was that he might be cured by psychotherapy. The third was that he might stay Uranian for the rest of his life. My job was to get him to accept this last possibility if it should prove to be the outcome, and adapt himself to it. He must learn to realize that the "world" was wrong in its total condemnation of Uranism, however right it may or may not be in its condemnation of physical homosexuality. Of course, I do not defend the seduction of minors, and I have no sympathy for the dissipated roué who turns to sodomy for a fresh thrill. But on the question of physical intimacy among persons like Edward I have to reserve my judgment. Of course he insisted on having my opinion. To have refused it would have been to have aroused all his fears again. So I said that at any rate I would not condemn it or him, but that my attitude in this was something like the regrettable attitude of St. Paul to hetero-sexual love—It is good for a man not to touch man, but if he *does* he should avoid fornication. That is to say, libertinism and promiscuity are as bad for the Uranian as for the "normal" man. And whatever Edward's own feelings on the subject may be, it is illegal, and heavy penalties are attached to it.

I didn't say these things at once. First of all I had to convince him (which was far from easy) that however much others had condemned him, we at Hawkspur really did approve him, before he could really begin to believe anything I told him. And over a period of eighteen months we were gradually able to get him to see that he had no cause for shame or guilt, and now he is able to accept himself as what he is, and his conflict is at any rate resolved sufficiently for him to be able to apply himself to the problem of earning a living—which he is doing very successfully

He was not by any means the only one of his kind—in fact as I have described him he is not, for obvious reasons, one at all, but an amalgam of two or three.

Very different was Cuthbert Parsons. He was much older than Edward, and our task was correspondingly more difficult. Brought up in a very religious atmosphere, the conflict that was set up in his mind as a result of his shockingly immoral tendencies was such as to demand an immediate and radical solution. He easily found one. He just repressed the whole conflict into unconsciousness and pretended it wasn't there. He allowed himself to admit that he was "interested in youngsters" and tried with a certain measure of success to obtain work among boys, so that he could adopt a strictly paternal attitude to them. His feelings of guilt and the whole conflict situation he rigidly repressed. But where there is guilt-feeling it cries out for punishment. He could not be punished for the "sin" which made him feel guilty because he had only committed it, so to speak, "in his own heart." But punished he must be, so he just did things which caused him to be punished; and he generally committed those crimes when he was most enjoying himself among a crowd of boys. That is to say, when he was enjoying the forbidden fruit he had to seek punishment, though sometimes he merely ran away, with or without someone else's funds. This man, even more than Edward, needed to resolve his conflict, accept himself for what he was, and see that society and not himself was in the wrong. We did not succeed with him because whenever the psychotherapist began to get him to face the dreadful fact, he just ran away. He came back two or three times, but I am afraid he will just go on punishing himself. He is another victim of this society which punishes people because they are ill.

The attitude, on the part of society, of shocked and dignified silence is one of the most potent causes of the most sordid kind of homosexuality. Another lad, in much the same position as Edward, being distressed and worried about himself, but being able to get no help or understanding from any of those whose job it was to help him, *did* one day find someone who understood him. Someone who understood him too well! It was in a part of London notorious for homosexuality. Our boy was listening to a tub-thumper when he got into conversation with a very friendly man, who took him to his flat for a cup of tea. He soon learned that there is nothing unusual about being homosexual, and if we had not got hold of him fairly soon he would certainly have become a professional Nancyboy. I am happy to say that he misappropriated quite a lot of his "friend's" property, and even began to think about a little blackmail. There is no excuse for this seducing of boys; but equally is there no excuse for the attitude of a society which compels these lads to go to unprincipled rogues for sympathy and understanding. That is the way more unprincipled rogues come into being.

There is still much division of opinion as to the cause of Uranism. Freud, if I understand him aright, attributes it to the mother fixation. Others have other ideas, and many think it is congenital. Perhaps all the suggested causes operate in different cases. But all who have given any thought to the subject are agreed on one point—that the deliberate pervert is a comparative rarity, and nothing could be more cruel, more unjust, and more indicative of ignorance, than the habit of classing the genuine Uranian or invert with the conscious pervert. Many want most desperately to be able to love in the same way as other men. Others—having faced the problem bravely and intelligently—are quite content to be as they are, and cannot understand anyone wanting to fall in love with a woman any more than you, dear reader, want to fall in love with someone of your own sex. But they are only slightly less unhappy than their dissatisfied fellows, because they are ringed around with suspicion, dare not indulge thousands of perfectly natural and innocent impulses, dare not even shake hands without wondering whether they are holding the other's hand too long, dare not indulge in a casual brotherly caress, or link arms in a friendly way, lest the strength of the emotion behind the act be divined and suspicion aroused. There is no need for these people—most of them refined and cultured far above the average—to be tortured from puberty to senescence. Perhaps one day society will learn what it owes to these men—and women—who, denied normal outlets for their emotions, have diverted their love and energy to the advancement of art and culture and learning, and the service of their fellows. And perhaps then the persecution will end.

CHAPTER THIRTEEN

"The course of true God never did run smooth"
SAMUEL BUTLER

Religion

It was a winter's night. Black outside, wet and cold. Inside there was no accumulator for the wireless because Camp Council was out of funds. For the same reason there were no table-tennis balls. Four people were playing a desultory game of cards. The others were huddled round the "tortoise" stove weary after a day of idleness, for this was Sunday. It was all very depressing. I had just returned from a "White House Tea Party" (we had two or three boys to tea at our house in the village every Sunday), where we had been talking about religion, and I said the first thing that came into my head . . . "Henry, my boy"—to the dullest of them all—"give us in a few well-chosen sentences *your* conception of the nature of God."

"Eh?"

I repeated it.

"Don't know watcher talkin abaht."

"Well, what do you think God is like?"

HENRY: "There ain't no God."

WILLS: "Ah! A categorical denial. Henry, you're an atheist. Lots of very clever people think you're wrong. But then, again, lots of other people, who are every bit as clever, think you're quite right." Which pleased Henry exceedingly, because, being a dull farmer's boy, he simply loved to be thought clever. He had lived close to nature in its cruder forms, and, though a lovable soul, was rather a crude form himself.

WILLS: Well, I see we shan't get much change out of you. If there ain't none you can't describe him.

TERENCE: God is not mocked.

(Terence, one of our oldest members, was an ardent R.C. A gentle, attractive character, he shortly afterwards developed the delusion that he was a well-known R.C. member of the nobility, and had to be translated to another sphere.)

WILLS: So you think there *is* one, do you, Terence? What's he like?

TERENCE: God is not mocked.

WILLS: I'm not mocking God, nor asking you to. I'm asking you what he's like.

TERENCE: He sits enthroned on high surrounded by Cherubim and Seraphim.

WILLS: Yes, but what's he *like?*

TERENCE: The most holy God is a mystery. You can't describe a mystery.

WILLS: Look. You're a Catholic surrounded by a lot of heretical unbelievers. Catholics are among the few people who know in whom they have believed. Now, come on. Tell us the Catholic view of God.

TERENCE: We are not encouraged to enter into arguments with heretics. But God is not mocked.

WILLS: Oh, I'm sorry. I don't want you to do anything against your religion. What about you, A.B.?

A.B. was a lad of 18 with a rather harsh father who, while he was conscientious, owned himself defeated by A.B., who was indolent and a pilferer. We cured him of both weaknesses.

A.B.: What about me?

WILLS: This is the Sabbath Day and we are keeping it holy by discussing the nature of God. Cough up your ideas.

A.B.: Haven't any.

WILLS: Nonsense. Everyone has them. Do you think there *is* a God?

A.B.: I guess so.

WILLS: Well—what about him?

A.B.: He made Heaven and earth.

WILLS: Some people say they just growed, like Topsy.

A.B.: Well, it had to get started, didn't it?

WILLS: Good enough. The predisposing cause, as the highbrows might say. What else?

A.B.: Search me.

WILLS: That's what I am doing. Come on, you know more about God than that.

A.B.: He shall come to judge the quick and the dead.

WILLS: An Anglican, I see.

A.B.: A what?

WILLS: C. of E.

A.B.: Not me. I don't belong to anything.

WILLS: No? Why not?

A.B.: All a lot of boloney.

WILLS: But you say there is a God. Is he a lot of boloney?

A.B.: Oh, how the hell should I know?

WILLS: Hell. Yes. I suppose that's where you'll go when, as quick or dead, God has judged you, is it?

A.B.: Not me. No such place.

WILLS: No?

A.B.: No. A lot of boloney. All these bloody parsons tell you God loves everybody and then they say he sends you to hell. A lot of boloney.

WILLS: I think you're right. I don't think a loving God would punish anyone. But mind *you*, I think he's taken the trouble to tell us how we can be happy, and if we don't take his advice we're apt to be miserable. That's hell enough for me. How about you, Raymond?

Raymond was a charming youth of 17 who had been pronounced incorrigible by his father and a long succession of foster-parents and schoolmasters, his mother having died when he was a baby. Gentle, sensitive (perhaps too sensitive), a natural æsthete, we are able to open his eyes to the world of beauty, and he is now getting on well in one of the artistic professions. He had been to tea with us.

RAYMOND: My idea of God isn't a bit like A.B.'s, but it used to be when I was a kid. If there is a God at all I think we see him in anything that is beautiful like a beautiful picture or lovely music.

WILLS: Like the soldier that Baden-Powell writes about who stood on top of a hill in South Africa beholding the kingdoms of the world and the glory of them, and said "who says there ain't no bloody God?"

RAYMOND: Sniff (he was already enough an æsthete of the less natural kind to scorn a relative Philistine like Baden-Powell).

WILLS: Well, it's the same idea, whether you like the comparison or not. And I may say it's a view I share, though I don't think it's a complete or comprehensive idea. Do you know that thing of Joseph Mary Plunkett's? You must have heard me reading it at poetry—"I see His blood upon the rose, and in the stars the glory of His eyes"?

RAYMOND: Yes, it's lovely.

WILLS: While we're among the ineffectual intellectuals, what about you, Adrian?

Adrian was about 21, tall, willowy, a shade effeminate, with strong artistic leanings, but who had not yet decided what was his medium. He found life at the camp a great burden, but at least he learned to make his own bed while he was with us.

ADRIAN: I think I share Raymond's view. I think if God can be given a personality and human attributes, he is a loving God. . . . But perhaps God is very much what we make him?

DICK: Hell! How can God be what we make him? Didn't he bloody well make us?

WILLS: Good for you, Adrian. The high spot so far. Remember the Israelites, Dicky? Or perhaps they were before your time. They thought God was a God of battle. "Slay the Amalakites, smite them hip and thigh, slay all the women and children, leave not a blade of corn standing . . ." all that sort of thing. Later, they thought he was a God of justice. Later still they thought he was a God of mercy—Hosea, was it, that gave them that idea? Then Jesus came along and said "God is more than that even. He is a God of love." We haven't really accepted that idea yet—we're still, in the main, worshipping one of the early Israelitish Gods. . . .

DICK: Don't know what the bloody hell you're talking about. (Bursting into song) "Jesus loves me this I know, for the Bible tells me so." Come on, let's have a service. "Will you come to the mission, will you come, will you come?" . . .

This Dick was, when he was not blaspheming, an ardent evangelical, and used to write turgid letters to his old Bible

Class leader all about the blood of the lamb. The other chaps used to egg him on to hold "open-air meetings" in the day-room, and before we knew where we were Dick was on the table conducting the singing of what he called his signature tune—"Bring them in, bring them in, bring them in from the fields of sin; Bring them in, bring them in, bring the sinners in to Jesus . . ."

After a riotous quarter of an hour we settled down again.

WILLS: Hold tight while I put the cocoa water on. (The nightly job of the Staff member on duty was to make the supper cocoa—on the same "tortoise" stove—and wash up afterwards. It was a job we had taken on voluntarily, so that the orderlies could go out if they wanted to.) Don't knock it over, you clumsy oaf. Now then, Tom. With a name like yours you should be an agnostic.

TOM: All right, Duke. I know! Doubting Thomas, eh? You see I know my Bible.

(Tom was sixteen, and I had a very soft spot for him, though he was violent, excitable, and suspicious, and we eventually lost him to a mental hospital.)

WILLS: And what do you gather from your Bible? About God, I mean.

TOM: Well, I don't think much of him.

WILLS: Which of the various Gods in the Bible don't you think much of?

TOM: None of 'em. Take Jesus. Says God is love. If God is love, why does he allow wars? Why do we have to die? Why are some people half-starved all their lives, and some have so much money they don't know what to do with it all?

WILLS: Are these questions intended to be purely rhetorical?

TOM: You can answer 'em if you know how, Duke.

WILLS: I don't profess to be able to answer them all fully and satisfactorily. I agree with Terence so far that God (if any) is a mystery, and therefore not wholly susceptible to human explanation. If he were wholly comprehensible he would not be God. But if I were anxious to defend God against your charges I think I could put up a case.

TOM: Go ahead.

WILLS: I could point you perhaps to Swinburne's *Hertha* . . . "I have need not of prayer, I have need of you free, as your mouths of mine air, that my heart may be greater within me, beholding the fruits of me fair" . . . within pretty broad limits man is free to build Jerusalem in England's green and pleasant land, or make it a little hell on earth. The fact that we have made it rather a hell than a heaven is only God's fault in so far as he made us free . . . a little lower than the angels. . . . I personally would rather be free to make mistakes, and learn from them, than be bound and incapable of them. I believe in freedom, whether at Hawkspur Camp or in the world at large. God has made me free, and anyone who tries to limit my freedom, whether it's a Hitler or a vindictive penal code, is going against God's will, is mocking God, if Terence will allow me to say so. This place would be a dashed sight more efficient, more clean, more industrious, if I were a little dictator. But we're sacrificing efficiency to the valuable experience of learning by our mistakes. Perhaps God has some such idea. I don't know . . . it's all very puzzling . . . But that's as good an hypothesis as any, don't you think. . . . Certainly it's that fact that we have abused our freedom that has made such a mess of things in the world at large. Whether such freedom is worth having is a question every man must decide for himself. Personally, I'm all for it.

TOM (who is a cynic): Give me liberty or give me death. I don't think. Give me a good dinner, a good bed, and a wench, and you can have your liberty.

WILLS: Let us not become bawdy. Perhaps a cup of cocoa would do you in the meantime. Shift your great carcase and I'll make it. Hurry up, the water's boiling. I am free, being bigger (though not fatter) than you, to give you a kick in the pants to hurry you up. But I refrain, so why be cynical about freedom? Some of us know how to use it! Here endeth the first lesson. What a session we've had. Like a meeting of the convocation of bishops, whatever that is.

So we had our bread and cheese and cocoa. But we could not leave the hare I had raised, and the discussion continued, sometimes getting quite heated, until lights out at eleven—and then, I understood, it was continued in the bunk-houses. Several more gave their conception of the nature of God and almost all were cynical, critical, or frankly primitive and anthropomorphic, envisaging an omnipotent God whose chief function was to inhibit freedom and punish the offenders.

Had they been better informed, or a little more capable of reasoning, they would have seen that the cynicism and disbelief were not so much of God as of his professional interpreters and their organizations. No parson would have been able to get anywhere near them. They had somehow acquired a distorted view of Christianity and they thought (rightly or wrongly) that their distorted views came from the mouths of the professional Christians. I am very much afraid they were not far wrong. But with me they were able to speak freely and fearlessly because (except in fun) I never used any language but their own, never professed to be anything intrinsically different from themselves, and never stood on a pedestal. Above all, I had never urged anyone to go to church, nor tried to force upon them anything in the nature of religious observance. One or two, from time to time, came to Friends' meeting with my wife and me, but that was, I fear, more because they liked us than because they liked our religion.

When I was a Settlement Warden in South Wales I had an interesting conversation with a young man—an intelligent young man who was studying law. After a little humming and hawing, he said: "er—I suppose you don't believe in God, do you?" "What," I said, "me, not believe in God? What makes you think that?" "Well," he said, "you're a Quaker, aren't you?" "Yes," I said. "Exactly." "Well . . . aren't Quakers atheists?" It was a shocking condemnation of my sect as well as of me personally, and it taught me a valuable lesson. While I still do believe that one's life and conduct should be the best sermon one can preach; and while on the other hand I am terribly nervous about spoken sermons, I do try to let the Hawkspurians see that I have some definite religious belief, though I always avoid orthodox ways of expressing it. And when at last we had gone the round on that winter's night, and it came to my turn, and they said, "Come on, Duke, you made all of us say, now you have *your* turn, I was not afraid to tell them what I thought. I told them that we all know of the existence of phenomena other then the tangible and ponderable—things like beauty and love. These things, I said, were emanations of the divine and had their place in all of us. Each of us is "a God, though in the germ." In each of us "nestles the seed of perfection." Thus are we sons of God and brothers of one another. Thus is it that we have before all other duties a duty of love to one another. This duty makes all hatred, all violence impossible to the true Christian. With this love Jesus cured the sick and healed those whose minds were disordered. This love was his "treatment" for the harlot, the publican, and the sinner whom he counted among his friends. I told them all this because, in my mind, this was the fundamental basis of all that I was trying to do at Hawkspur Camp. We have still not accepted Christ's teaching, and now after two thousand years we are hearing it afresh from the mouths of agnostic psychiatrists. They are telling us that there can be no effective cure for any of the things we are concerned with at Hawkspur Camp (and many other things in the world at large) without love. They do not use those words. Indeed they express themselves, very often, in a way that is repellent to many respectable people, and once again the gospel is being rejected. But one day we must come to it.

CHAPTER FOURTEEN

Conclusion

"... So What?"

ANY AMERICAN

At the time the discussions on the ill-fated Criminal Justice Bill were at their height, the Howard League for Penal Reform called a conference at Caxton Hall to discuss several amendments which seemed to them desirable. One thing which was causing them grave concern was the proposal that summary courts should be given the power to send a boy to Borstal. One of the arguments advanced in favour of this proposal ran to the effect that Borstal was such an admirable form of training that it was a pity to deprive so many boys of the opportunity of undergoing it, simply because of the arbitrary chance of their having committed an offence triable at a summary court. I ventured to reply to this argument. I said that Borstal might very well be all that was claimed for it. In that case a happy compromise suggested itself to me. I believe that very few young offenders want to become habitual criminals (and here I return to where I started—they are all "good boys really"). If they can find a clear way out of the mess they are in they will usually take it. They will not jib at Borstal if Borstal is going to put them on their feet. So why not make it voluntary? The magistrates could explain the circumstances to them, and ask them whether they would not like to go to Borstal and be put on their feet again. Nearly everyone who comes to Hawkspur Camp comes voluntarily, well knowing that they will have to endure in many ways far worse rigours than are endured at Borstal, with its central heating, electric light, sports fields, separate rooms, and what not. I believe that very many would accept Borstal.

"Mr. Wills," said Mrs. Clara Rackham afterwards, "I did not know you could be so sarcastic." "I haven't been sarcastic," I said. And neither had I. It was a perfectly sound proposition, and it still is—though it may have seemed somewhat sarcastic to assume that many youths would accept Borstal as at present constituted. I was merely assuming the rosiest pictures of Borstal life to be true ones. I believe firmly that if Borstal has one outstanding failing, it is to be found in that element of compulsion which runs through the whole thing, based on the assumption that the young criminal does not want to be cured. Of course, many will say that they intend to go on in their careers, especially if society is going out of its way to make things unpleasant for them. It is difficult to convince anyone that you are really anxious to help him if you adopt a stern, condemnatory attitude, and tell him that he deserves to have things made hot for him, and you are jolly well going to do it. That is the very thing that is likely to change a boastful threat into a stern resolve. The youngster says he's going to go on in the same old way, just to show he's not frightened of you; and later on he carries on in the same old way, to get his own back. Some magistrates and judges think they have failed if they do not make the prisoner cringe before them. But if society could get rid of its vindictive, punitive attitude, and adopt instead an attitude of "What a mess you're in—let's see if between us we can get you out of it"—what a difference we should find. We want something more of the attitude of the Quaker who, when he had a gun pointed at his head on a lonely moor, placed his hand on his assailant's shoulder and said: "My dear man! Whatever has brought you to this?"

I do not suggest for one moment that all our state institutions for the treatment of adolescent offenders can be run on precisely the same lines as Hawkspur Camp. Hawkspur Camp is for the beginners. Others—as I have said—have to be kept in confinement especially during the early stages of treatment. Properly approached I believe that many will even accept coercion voluntarily, paradoxical as this may seem. But they are only likely to accept it if they are genuinely being offered *treatment*, and not merely detention. And, indeed, it is very difficult to carry out a real treatment unless it is in large measure voluntary, as the co-operation of the "patient" makes things infinitely easier.

Nor do I think, of course, that Hawkspur Camp achieved perfection. It was hampered and crippled from beginning to end by a chronic lack of funds, and by complete absence of official recognition. When I made tentative approaches to the Home Office about recognition as a Probation Home or Hostel I was received very kindly, but was told, very politely, that we should have to have much more "discipline" before we could ever be recognized by them. Though that was not the official reason for refusing it—the official reason was some obscure piece of red tape which I do not even recall, but which made us ineligible even to apply! But I believe that at Hawkspur Camp there was the germ of an idea, an idea which will have to spread if we are to see a real step forward in our treatment of this problem.

In the early days of the camp we were visited by Mr. G. Clutton-Brock, now Warden of Oxford House, but then Principal Probation Officer for the London Area. His final remark, as he picked his way through the morass at our entrance was "All you need now, Wills, is £10,000." I repeated this remark afterwards to Jim Payne, who said: "If Hawkspur Camp had £10,000 it would be ruined." Both were right. Money spent lavishly would quite eliminate the pioneering aspect of the camp, but ten thousand pounds could be used very effectively and I have had many day-dreams about how I would use it. I would eliminate the maintenance fee, so that the camp could be open to all who need it instead of only to those who can pay at least fifteen shillings a week. I would have a site on which there were permanent buildings as a nuclear *pied-à-terre*, but which also had a wooded portion where real pioneering could always be carried on. Many people destroy because they simply don't know how to construct. Smashing and building, like love and hate, are much the same thing really. I would realize an ambition which I was never able to begin to realize at Hawkspur—I would have a corner of the site set apart for the completely lawless and unco-operative, where they could do just exactly as they pleased until they had made the place too uncomfortable to live in—then they could stay in it until they had made it comfortable again. The place would not often be occupied, but when it was, I or one of my most trusted colleagues would also be there, watching, but never interfering. I do not think it is possible to teach a trade in a "corrective" establishment. In Borstal everyone has a chance to start learning something, but the conditions are bound to be artificial, and very few ex-Borstalians, I am told, follow the trade they were taught at Borstal. That is one reason why we have never professed to teach trades—our aim is only to learn to live together. Nevertheless, I would like to have been able to see greater diversity of jobs available than we had at Hawkspur, and if I had Clutton-Brock's £10,000 I would certainly expand somewhat on those lines. I have always wanted to have an old car that could be taken to pieces and put together again for the fun (and instruction) of the thing. We have had our old cars, but they were for use, and anyway they didn't need taking to pieces—they just fell apart.

I would employ a full-time psychiatric social worker whose job it would be to write up, from personal contact with parents, teachers, etc., a full social history for each boy, and then keep in touch with the parents until the lad was on his feet again. If he (or she) had any time left over after all this he would also be responsible for finding jobs for "leavers."

The site of our camp would I think be within easier reach of London and the Institute for the Scientific Treatment of Delinquency (I.S.T.D.) than Hawkspur Camp. The I.S.T.D. has been absolutely invaluable to us. It has "vetted" all our cases, giving complete physical and psychometric examinations as well as a psychiatric interview before ever a boy was accepted. Once at the camp, the I.S.T.D. provided, from its rota of practitioners, psychotherapy where it was needed, and a thousand and one other things. One boy is too fat—the I.S.T.D. arranges for a noted endocrinologist to treat him; another boy has a squint—the I.S.T.D. gets him into a hospital to have it removed; another needs glasses—I.S.T.D. arranges it—and so on. It is a wonderful institution. I do not know what we should have done without it, and the support of one of its most energetic directors, Dr. Denis Carroll. But it was a long way off, and we ought to be nearer to it.

But perhaps it is £100,000 we need. And why not? As I write we are spending every day in destroying people enough money to keep in perpetuity all the Hawkspur Camps this country needs. For it does need many. I suggest that when we start reconstructing after the war, if the powers that be do not want to apply the voluntary principle to Borstal, then they should offer "beginners" the opportunity of going to a Q Camp—and provide funds to make it possible to keep such places running. One of the dire consequences which will follow the levelling down of incomes with which we are threatened after the war, is that it will eliminate the class which, by its munificent gifts, keeps voluntary organizations alive. This means that there will have to be more spending of public money on experimental ventures, and, unless social experiment is to die altogether, a much greater measure of freedom must be given with the money than is possible with our present method of spending public money.

Social progress in this country has always begun with private effort, financed by the well-to-do. The State has "taken over" these concerns if and when they proved their usefulness. If the well-to-do are to be eliminated we shall need as a State a much bolder social policy than the country has seen yet.

But we, as a people, must change our attitude to our criminals for another and bigger reason than that. We are now at war, we are told, for the preservation of certain moral principles—freedom, democracy, and what not—the kind of virtues that are usually associated with what is sometimes known as Christian civilization. I personally do not believe that war is any way of preserving these things, but I am not so pessimistic as to believe that war must permanently destroy them.

If we wish to preserve them, and if we wish to avoid future wars (for they cannot exist together), our whole social order, I firmly believe, must be moulded in its internal as well as in its international aspects, to be much more in keeping with the teachings of Jesus. How this may be done in other spheres is not here my concern. How it may be done in the treatment of society's misfits I have been here trying to show.

I am well aware that it is considered a very elementary mistake to confuse crime with sin. Sin, we are told, is an affair between a man and his Maker; crime is an affair between a man and society. God's way with sinners is the way of love and forgiveness. It will take a great deal to convince me that God's way with those who offend against his laws is of no avail when used by us with those who offend against ours.

There is no ambiguity, no equivocation, about the commandment that we must love our neighbour, and I do not read anywhere in the Scriptures that we are excused from that duty if our neighbour steals our gold watch, or has a bad temper. Of course we may have to restrain our neighbour sometimes, even as we have to restrain those of unsound mind, or as we have to isolate people with infectious diseases. But I contend that this can be done—as it never is done to-day—in a spirit of love and sympathy, as it is done with the sick and insane.

I would remove completely any suggestion of retribution or punishment from our penal system, and replace it with an attitude of scientific detachment concerned only with bringing about a "cure." But it must also be an attitude that is informed by a spirit of love—not only because modern science is at last discovering that love, more than any other one thing, is of vital importance in the healing of those who are socially maladjusted; but because we profess to be a Christian nation, and that is the way of Christ.

Index

For Product Safety Concerns and Information please contact our EU representative GPSR@taylorandfrancis.com
Taylor & Francis Verlag GmbH, Kaufingerstraße 24, 80331 München, Germany

www.ingramcontent.com/pod-product-compliance
Lightning Source LLC
Chambersburg PA
CBHW050446280326
41932CB00013BA/2256
* 9 7 8 1 0 3 2 3 8 0 5 2 0 *